CATCH A
THIEF

TO CATCH A THIEF

Robert Tilton

Robert Tilton Ministries
Dallas, Texas

Unless otherwise indicated, all Scripture quotations are taken from the King James Version of the Bible.

Scripture quotations marked (NIV) are taken from the Holy Bible, New International Version. Copyright © 1973, 1978, 1984 International Bible Society. Used by permission of Zondervan Bible Publishers.

Verses marked TLB are taken from *The Living Bible*, copyright 1971 by Tyndale House Publishers, Wheaton, IL. Used by permission.

TO CATCH A THIEF
ISBN 0-914307-22-3
Copyright © 1984 by Word of Faith Publishing
Revised Printing March, 1988

Published by Robert Tilton Ministries
P. O. Box 819000, Dallas, Texas 75381-9000
Printed in the United States of America
All Rights Reserved
No Reproduction Without Permission
Editor: Kathryn P. Ingley
Cover Design by Kim Kreilaus

Contents

But if he [the thief] be found, he shall restore sevenfold; he shall give all the substance of his house. Proverbs 6:31 (NIV)

	Preface	7
I.	Identify Your Enemy	15
II.	Stand on the Word	21
III.	Conquer Fear	27
IV.	Change Your Thinking	43
V.	Examine the Thief's Origin	49
VI.	Return to God, Legally	55
VII.	Find Your Position in Christ	61
VIII.	Abide in His Love	67
IX.	Be What God Created You to Be	73
X.	Pursue Your Dreams	85
XI.	Establish Your Goals	95
XII.	Regain Your Possessions	109
XIII.	Refuse Limitations	115
XIV.	Expect a Sevenfold Return	125
XV.	Act Upon God's Word	139
XVI.	Catch the Thief	147

Preface

The thief stole $12,000-worth from Joann; but he couldn't keep it. God returned it all (and more) to her!

Around two o'clock in the morning, a thief stole over $12,000 in jewels and clothes, along with a sales appointment book from Joann's car. She had just returned from a trip and had not yet unpacked the car.

Joann is a single woman who sells credit services to major corporations. Her appointment book was vital to her because it contained all the information on her accounts and all her appointments for the next six months.

With only six days to meet her quota at the time her appointment book was stolen, her chances looked dim; but without her appointment book it looked impossible. Unless she met her quota, she would be put on probation.

She immediately cried out to God for help, asking that the book be returned within 24 hours. She bound the devil and loosed her things from his grasp; she commanded that they be returned sevenfold. Then Joann and two friends searched the area alleys, but they found nothing.

Afterwards, physically tired and emotionally drained, Joann returned home. As she continued to pray, she realized that the enemy was trying to attack her through her emotions. Immediately, she began to reflect on what God had done in her life. She thanked God for her salvation and for the many miracles He had already given her. She realized that things do not matter.

"I told the devil I resented his trying to get to me through this theft; and I told him I *have* my appointment book through faith in Jesus' Name. Then I refused to think about it anymore."

The next morning, Joann called her daughter, Maggie, who prayed and rebuked the enemy, demanding that he return Joann's appointment book immediately! Maggie then felt the Lord strongly impress her to call her husband, Fred, who was on vacation at home.

Fred and Maggie had already defeated the devil that day at 5 a.m. as I had taught them to do. So as Maggie explained to Fred about the burglary, the Lord spoke to him in a still, small voice, "It's in a garbage dumpster."

Fred went immediately to Joann's house where he asked what was in the car, what the luggage looked like, and where the burglary had taken place. Before he left, he and Joann agreed as Fred prayed with authority that her possessions would be found. Then he left saying he was going to get the things.

These folks tithe and give offerings; they know what it is to come off the bottom of square one with God. God said if we make Him our Source of help, worship Him with tithes, offerings and vows, He will rebuke the devourer.

God told Fred the stolen things were in a dumpster, but He didn't tell Fred which one.

- Do you have any idea how many dumpsters are in Dallas?
- Do you know what is inside one? Garbage!

Fred combed the neighborhood alleys and checked behind buildings for dumpsters.

- He went to the first one; the things were not there.
- He went to the second one; the things were not there.

In 105-degree heat, Fred climbed in and out of one dozen dumpsters—no diamonds, no jewelry, no clothes, and no appointment book!

Then he searched the second dozen and no jewelry. He climbed in and out of those hot, filthy garbage dumpsters. I remember when I saw Fred, he looked like garbage from the top of his head to the bottom of his feet.

Imagine how tempted he was to quit. I'm sure the devil [the thief] was telling Fred, "You're foolish. It's over 100 degrees out here and it stinks! Fred, go home and enjoy your vacation. You'll never find Joann's things in all of the thousands of dumpsters in Dallas."

However, Fred had heard a Word from God and faith had risen in his heart. He knew he would succeed if he didn't stop. Then in the 36th dumpster, among the dirty diapers from a nearby nursery, Fred found Joann's appointment book, jewelry, and clothes. Only the makeup case was missing, and he found that in the driveway where trucks had run over it.

In less than 12 hours after the theft, Fred had recovered everything except for two relatively inexpensive earrings which apparently had fallen out.

With the return of her appointment book, Joann went on to exceed her sales quota. Her insurance took care of cleaning and repairing her clothes and jewelry, and replacing her makeup, which was an immediate sevenfold return. Even one of the inexpensive earrings was replaced.

The only thing left unreplaced is an earring Joann bought in Hawaii several years ago. So, what does God do? He gives her a free trip for two to Hawaii to get that earring replaced! Isn't it something the way God forces Satan to restore what he steals from God's children who trust totally in God?

Joann, Fred and Maggie believe Joann received a sevenfold return. No one knows how God computes a sevenfold return, but the Bible does say that God chooses the foolish things of this world to confound the wise. When Joann reported the recovery to her local chief of police, she asked why the police hadn't searched the dumpsters as Fred had.

The chief peered at Joann keenly and chuckled, "There would be no way we would think to look in dumpsters because thieves don't throw items in the dumpster. If they're getting rid of them, they take them down to the river or someplace and dump them. They *never* use dumpsters."

A kind man with many years of service, he told Joann that in all of his years with the department he had never heard of anything like this. He said it was inconceivable that the thief didn't keep the fine jewelry.

It may not be a garbage dumpster you are digging through; you may be digging through the hassles of life. At sometime you asked God to help and direct you, and He will if you don't faint. As you dig through the garbage, stay in faith and don't doubt; and you will find what was stolen from you. I think this is one of the most remarkable stories I have ever heard—36 garbage dumpsters!

You, too, have an adversary [Satan] who wants to steal your life, marriage, finances, and your health. He doesn't want you to be successful or to do anything for God; he wants you snivelling in the corner, beaten up by life, fainting, giving up, and ready to commit suicide.

But Jesus wants you to stay in faith, to catch the thief [Satan], and to force him to restore the things he has stolen from you.

I have written this book to teach you how to live according to the Bible and how to catch the thief in your life. I have written this book to help you become all God created you to be.

Let's Pray

Father, I believe Your Word is like seed planted in good ground. It will produce much fruit.

Lord, let this prayer break the powers of darkness off the readers of this book. Let the scales fall from their eyes and let them see what You created them to be. Let them see that they are created in Your image and that You came to bring them abundant life.

Lord, let them see that Satan comes like a thief to steal from them their money, their dreams, their happiness and their families. In this book, let me expose Satan's devices in the Name of Jesus and pull down his strongholds. Let me break his shackles off every believer.

Thank You, Lord, for what You are about to do as we study Your Word. I believe You for miracles now, in Jesus' Name, Amen.

1

Identify Your Enemy

Because of your lack of knowledge, Satan steals your money, your dreams, your happiness, and your family.

Satan, like a thief, roams the earth looking for innocent victims. He looks for people who are not watching and people who are naive to his wicked devices, so that he can steal from them. He is an adversary to your faith; and if he can get his hands on your possessions without your knowing it, he will. Then he endeavors to keep you from finding out about it.

He doesn't want you to get smart and light your lamp like the five wise virgins did

(Matthew 25:1-12). Instead, he wants you to walk in darkness. He wants to keep your eyes blinded.

He wants you to keep acknowledging the "old man," instead of putting on the "new man." He wants to:

- defeat you
- destroy your marriage
- destroy your business
- bankrupt you, and
- force you to die a premature death

But we are going to catch that thief in your life and make him restore to you those things he has stolen.

> But if he [the thief] is caught, he must pay sevenfold, though it costs him all the wealth of his house.
>
> Proverbs 6:31 (NIV)

Make a commitment to soak yourself in the teachings in this book. The Lord told me that every chapter will be a therapeutic process of changing you, strengthening you, and standing you up on your feet.

Some of you will be delivered from cancer as you read and study. Healing is available, and your faith will be built to receive your healing. However, these teachings are not "instant." You must pay attention, study, review, and let the Word of God open your eyes. There is a special anointing upon the truth that I am opening up to you, but it is not magic. IT'S MIRACULOUS.

God wants us to be aware of Satan's devices, lest he get an advantage over us. Through our lack of knowledge, Satan [the thief] steals, kills, and destroys our lives.

> My people are destroyed for lack of knowledge. Hosea 4:6

Many people crawl through life because nobody ever told them they could stand on their feet and walk as God created them to walk. You may be crawling through life and not know it. God said His people are destroyed because of the lack of knowledge.

> The thief cometh not, but for to steal, and to kill, and to destroy: I am come that they might have life, and that they might have it more abundantly.
> John 10:10

In the earlier part of John 10, Jesus named Satan a thief and a robber. He comes to discourage you, to overcome you, and to stop you from having what God created you to have from the beginning.

In contrast, Jesus came that you might have life abundantly—a life of excellence, above the ordinary, great in quantity, more than sufficient, and plentiful.

Satan came to steal from you—to take your property or possessions, your position, and your purpose in this life and in the life to come.

Satan came to kill you and your faith. He attacks you with trials, tribulations, and distresses. He endeavors to overcome you because he wants you to give up and stop trying.

The devil has also come to destroy you—to deteriorate your life, to pull you down, and to discourage you from being whom God created you to be, from doing what God wants you to do, and from having what God created for you.

According to II Corinthians 2:11, you are not to be ignorant of Satan's devices, lest he get the advantage over you.

Through your lack of knowledge, Satan can get an advantage—dominion, power, authority, and control—over you. The thief can literally get control over your family, your marriage, your business, and your finances through your ignorance!

That's why God's Word says you are not to be ignorant of Satan's devices. Instead, you must gain information and knowledge from God's Word.

Put Knowledge in Place of the Unknown

A businessman who was seated next to me on an airplane recently kept fidgeting, so I asked him what was wrong. He told me that he was afraid of flying.

When I asked him what he was afraid of, he said he was afraid of the unknown. He was afraid because he didn't have control of the airplane.

He could have expanded his cosmetics business, but he was afraid to fly. Therefore, he expanded his business only as far as he could drive. It was rare for him to be in a plane.

That man had a successful business which didn't expand because of his fear of flying. The thief had used fear to stop the growth of the man's business.

I recently read about another person who was afraid of flying, but she decided to do something about it and went to flight school. As she gained knowledge of planes, the fear of flying left her. She is now breaking the majority of the records for women pilots; because through knowledge, she overcame the fear of flying.

The thief steals from you without your knowing it. That is why Proverbs 4:23 admonishes you to guard your heart with diligence, for out of it flows the issues [forces] of life. Literally, those forces of life coming out of your spirit-man can produce good or evil. The stuff that life is made of comes out of your heart.

> A good man out of the good treasure of the heart bringeth forth good things: and an evil man out of the evil treasure bringeth forth evil things.
> Matthew 12:35

Although Satan used fear to steal life from humanity, you can catch the thief and conquer fear.

> Ye shall know the truth, and the truth shall make you free.
>
> John 8:32

Through lack of knowledge, Satan gets an advantage over us; but through knowledge we take away his advantage. True knowledge comes only from the Word of God.

2

Stand on the Word

The Word is alive! Like a consuming fire, it thaws God's bigness in you and flattens the mountains Satan builds up.

The Bible tells of one of the most affluent and respected men in the East. He had thousands of goats, sheep, camels and a great family with many children and grandchildren. But Satan stole from him.

> And the Lord said unto Satan, Hast thou considered my servant Job, that there is none like him in the earth, a perfect and an upright man, one that feareth God, and escheweth evil?

> Then Satan answered the Lord, and said, Doth Job fear God for nought? Job 1:8-9

"Fearing the Lord" is not dread or apprehension of danger; it is having respect and reverential awe for God.

> Hast not thou made an hedge about him, and about his house, and about all that he hath on every side? thou hast blessed the work of his hands, and his substance is increased in the land.
>
> But put forth thine hand now, and touch all that he hath, and he will curse thee to thy face.
>
> And the Lord said unto Satan, Behold, all that he hath is in thy power; only upon himself put not forth thine hand. So Satan went forth from the presence of the Lord.
> Job 1:10-12

God told Satan that Job was in Satan's power. The only way Job could have been in the power of the devil was by Job choosing to yield himself to the power and the spirit of the devil.

There are three forms of power: the power of God, the power of the devil, and the power of man. The devil is a spirit, God is a spirit, and man is a spirit. Man's spirit yields to either God or to Satan; and to whomever you yield yourself, that is whose servant you become. So stay yielded to God.

For years, religionists have said God did all of this to Job. God did not do all of that to Job; it was the devil. Jesus said that the thief comes to steal, to kill, and to destroy; but, "I am come that they might have life, and that they might have it more abundantly" (John 10:10).

James 1:13 (NIV) tells us, "God cannot be tempted with evil, nor does he tempt anyone." Evil is anything that is contrary to good, anything morally wrong or wicked, anything causing ruin, injury, or pain. Is sickness evil? Is losing your family evil? If God is doing any tempting, testing, and trying, He is not doing it with sickness and disease; He is doing it with health.

Some people pray, "Lord, if it is Thy will, heal me." People who pray that way are showing their ignorance of the Word of God. God's Word clearly states it is the will of God to heal (III John 2). You should already know that because Jesus went about doing good, healing all that were oppressed of the devil (Matthew 4:23; 9:35).

The Word is alive. Like a consuming fire, it thaws out God's bigness inside you. It flattens the mountains which Satan has built up through fear. The Word moves the walls of Jericho [fear], causing them to fall down. Faith walks in and takes your inheritance for you.

Some people say, "What will be, will be." That is religious programming. If "what will be, will be,'' then we might as well go ahead and die and be with the Lord. However, if that were true, why did God give us the keys of prayer and the keys to the kingdom?

Why did God give us the power of attorney to use the Name of Jesus? He gave us this power so that we can PULL DOWN THE DEVIL'S STRONGHOLDS AND RELEASE THE BLESSINGS OF GOD INTO THE EARTH! Therefore, we will not let the devil get an advantage over us any more. We are going to pull down those strongholds that Satan has been programming us with for years.

Not long ago, I ministered on television to a woman whose legs had been numb for years. In a few seconds, those legs began to move and feeling came back into them. God healed her back, and she stood up unassisted for the first time in years. Why? Because we caught the thief in her life and forced him to restore the use of her legs.

What have you lost? Has the enemy stolen your health, money, job, or a deserved promotion? Have you lost a precious keepsake, the hope for a miracle, the dream of your heart, a loved one's affection, a house, or a car?

God has put it on my heart to help you supernaturally regain and recover whatever it is that has been taken from you.

When the thief took Joann's possessions, she called Maggie and Fred and they all agreed in prayer and expected a miracle. I had taught them four basic spiritual principles for catching the thief in their lives. You need to learn these principles now.

- **The power of agreement.**
  If two of you shall agree on earth as touching any thing that they shall ask, it shall be done for them of my Father which is in heaven.

  Matthew 18:19

- **Catching a thief.**
  If he [the thief] is caught, he must pay sevenfold, though it costs him all the wealth of his house.

  Proverbs 6:31 (NIV)

- **Paying vows.**
  Offer unto God thanksgiving; and pay thy vows unto the most High: and call upon me in the day of trouble: I will deliver thee, and thou shalt glorify me.   Psalm 50:14-15

- **Giving tithes and offerings.**
  Will a man rob God? Yet ye have robbed me. But ye say, Wherein have we robbed thee? In tithes and offerings.

  Ye are cursed with a curse: for ye have robbed me, even this whole nation.

> Bring ye all the tithes into the storehouse, that there may be meat in mine house, and prove me now herewith, saith the Lord of hosts, if I will not open you the windows of heaven, and pour you out a blessing, that there shall not be room enough to receive it.
>
> And I will rebuke the devourer for your sakes, and he shall not destroy the fruits of your ground; neither shall your vine cast her fruit before the time in the field, saith the Lord of hosts. Malachi 3:8-11

When the day of adversity came for Joann, Fred and Maggie, they were armed with the Word of God that I had taught them and were ready to defeat the enemy. They had learned to prove God with their tithes and offerings so that in the time of trouble they could draw upon God's ability (with clear conscience) to rebuke the devil and destroy his ugly thieving ways.

They put a demand on their faith; they released their faith by Fred's searching in the dumpsters. When he searched and searched without stopping, God caused the stolen things to be lying where he could spot them.

It is amazing what God will do for those who act in faith and trust totally in Him as their Source of supply.

3

Conquer Fear

Satan uses fear to kill, steal and destroy anyone who will listen to him. You must learn to recognize his tactics.

Job had a thief in his life. Matthew 12:34 says, "Out of the abundance of the heart the mouth speaketh." Job's mouth spoke his fears, and he opened the door thereby to the thief.

> For the thing which I greatly feared is come upon me, and that which I was afraid of is come upon me.
>
> I was not in safety, neither had I rest, neither was I quiet; yet trouble came.   Job 3:25-26

Fear will do this to you, also. Fear will bring you out of safety and expose you to trouble and destruction. Fear is the greatest enemy man can have in life. Job's fear was greater than his faith.

God did not give Job the spirit of fear! It is the devil, not God, who has the spirit of fear.

> For God hath not given us the spirit of fear; but of power, and of love, and of a sound mind.   II Timothy 1:7

> We having the same spirit of faith, according as it is written.
> II Corinthians 4:13

Confess this aloud: "The spirit of fear comes from the devil. I have the spirit of faith which comes from God."

Although fear is one of the greatest enemies in life, the Word of God gives you faith to overcome fear.

Fear daily keeps multitudes of people from being what God created them to be. The number one killer among adults is heart attacks. The Bible says that in the last days men's hearts shall fail them for fear (Luke 21:26). The fearful think continually of the worst things that could happen. Man literally worries himself to death.

When fear comes, your heart begins to pump faster and adrenalin is released into your body, just as God designed. Stress builds and your heart works double-time, eventually burning itself out.

Being anxious and fearful about a problem is like starting an avalanche. Fear sets chemicals loose in your body which goof up your thinking so much that you can develop mental or emotional illnesses. Far too many hospital beds are occupied by people who are ill because of the things they feared. Fear took control of their lives.

Over half of teenage deaths are suicide. The devil told them they had no reason to live, no purpose, and no position in life. So the thief stole their lives.

You have a purpose! You were not created to be nothing. You were created in the image of God to be something beautiful. You have a specific purpose from God in this earth. You are a part of God's kingdom.

Satan uses fear to kill, steal, and destroy anyone who will listen to him. You must learn to recognize fear and its functions.

Functions of Fear

Fear steals. Fear causes you to hesitate and stops you from moving out when God has a blessing for you. Fear comes to steal your possessions, your position, your purpose, and what God called you to do in this life.

Fear also steals faith. When you get excited about doing something, the devil tries to put fear into you by asking, *"What if* this?" or *"What if* that?" The first time you bought a nice car, the devil came along and said, "You'd better not buy that car! You will lose your job and won't be able to pay for it."

These "what ifs" are outward expressions of the fear that is inside an individual. Many people go through life afraid of the unknown, afraid of what they can't see. At night, some people leave lights on, because they're afraid of what they can't see in the dark.

The devil likes to keep you in the dark. The Bible says he is the god of this world, and he has blinded minds.

Fear is a destroyer.

> The thief cometh not, but for to steal, and to kill, and to destroy: I am come that they might have life, and that they might have it more abundantly.
> John 10:10

Since the thief uses fear against us, we can say, "Fear cometh not but for to steal, and to kill, and to destroy."

Fear works against you; but Jesus came to bring you abundant life. Who is Jesus? He is the Word of God who became flesh.

> And the Word was made flesh, and dwelt among us, (and we beheld his glory, the glory as of the only begotten of the Father,) full of grace and truth. John 1:14

Jesus, the living Word of God, came to earth and walked around among us.

> For this purpose the Son of God was manifested, that he might destroy the works of the devil.   I John 3:8

> In the beginning was the Word, and the Word was with God, and the Word was God.   John 1:1

Jesus and the Word are one. The Word produces faith, and Jesus (the Word, the *Logos*) is the Author and the Finisher of our faith (Hebrews 12:2). Therefore, faith comes by hearing the Word (Romans 10:17).

Thus we could read John 10:10 this way. *Fear* cometh not, but for to steal, and to kill, and to destroy: but *faith* came that you might have life, and that you might have it more abundantly.

> Now faith is the substance of things hoped for, the evidence of things not seen.   Hebrews 11:1

The New English Bible translation says, Faith "makes us certain of realities we do not see."

So fear takes life away from you, but faith gives it to you!

Fear expects the worst, but faith expects the best. You must expect the best and believe; then you will receive the best.

- **Faith says,** "Believe you will receive the best."

- **Fear says,** "Expect the worse."
- **Fear comes** to steal, to kill, and to destroy life.
- **Faith comes** to bring the reality of life to you.

Fear freezes life. It stops you from progressing toward what God created you for. It stops you from launching out into deeper experiences. It keeps your eyes on the ordinary. But Jesus says, "Look to Me; look to faith and see what it will do."

Fear freezes life, but faith thaws it. Abundant life wants to thaw healing in you, for the Healer lives inside you. Faith wants to thaw those creative, inspired ideas that are resident inside the incorruptible seed sown inside you. Faith thaws the dreams of what God created you to be.

Fear works against you. It tries to:

- Push you down
- Push you back
- Stop you
- Overcome you
- Discourage you
- Take your possessions away from you

> **FEAR WORKS AGAINST YOU.**
> **FAITH WORKS FOR YOU.**
> **FEAR STOPS LIFE.**
> **FAITH BRINGS LIFE.**

Faith came that you might have life, and have it more abundantly. Faith came that you might have a life superior in quality—above the ordinary, filled with excellence—the kind of life God created you to have.

For years, the thief stole from Marte and me. We barely got along because we feared each other. We even feared loving each other. We feared, so we couldn't trust each other. Fear came to take our lives, but faith came to give us life. Then faith, trust, and love began to build in our lives. Today I can say sincerely, "Marte, I love you, I love you, I love you. I'm glad I am delivered of fear. I love you."

The Matter of Priorities

A beautiful woman who was totally bound by fear watched Marte and me on television. She was so afraid that she wouldn't leave her house, not even to go grocery shopping. Because of her great fear, her marriage had fallen apart. She weighed only 90 pounds because she wouldn't eat.

Once, during a fight, she kicked her husband, who was chief of police in one of the suburbs of Dallas, and hurt her foot. Initially, because of her fear, she didn't go to the doctor. However, she couldn't bear the touch of sheets and blankets on her foot at night. Later the doctor told her the pain would always be there because her foot was so messed up.

Then one day, while watching us on television, she heard me say, "You are hurting, and I know you are hurting. I used to hurt, but I found out how not to hurt. I want to tell you how not to hurt."

That caught her attention, so she kept watching every day. "I got hooked immediately," she said during an interview, "because you were saying there was hope, and my life was hopeless. I had tried to kill myself twice. I knew something had to change. I was either going to leave my husband—and I couldn't do that because I couldn't leave the house—or I was going to kill myself or him because our fights were so violent.

"Then your television program came into my life, and I said, 'God, if you're real, I sure would like to see a sign.'

"Then you said, 'I see a woman sitting in her bedroom who wants to call. People have been mean to you all your life, and you're afraid to trust anybody.'

"I said, 'Wow! That could be me!' "

That woman was bound by fear. The thief had backed her off into a corner, but she began to hear the truth. She heard that Jesus wanted her to have life.

> Nor trust in uncertain riches, but in the living God, who giveth us richly all things to enjoy. I Timothy 6:17

While watching Marte and me on television, she found out that the thief was fear; and God set her free.

Don't trust in things you can see. Trust God, whom you cannot see, yet who giveth us all things to enjoy.

It's a matter of priorities. It's a matter of what you are looking at and to whom you are yielding yourselves as servants. Trust not in the things you can see because you cannot draw strength from visible things.

That woman, though bound by fear, called for help. Our prayer ministers prayed and broke the spirit of fear off her. She got saved, baptized in the Holy Ghost, and God healed her. When her husband came home, he immediately noticed something different. She shared with me how good it felt to walk out on the front steps of her home without being totally afraid. She said it was the most magnificent feeling to step out of the house for the first time in years without being bound by fear.

Her husband also committed his life to Christ and was filled with the baptism of the Holy Spirit.

Don't Listen to Words of Fear

Many years ago a student in a college mathematics class held down several jobs and was usually late to class. He came into class one day as the professor was putting two problems on the board. The professor said that whoever worked those problems would get one of two job openings.

This was during the depression, and this young man needed a better job. He went back to his house and worked all night, but he could only solve one problem. The next day in class he presented the solution of that one problem to the professor. The student was discouraged because he had wanted to work both of them.

The professor held up the piece of paper and said, "How did you work this? How did you get the solution? Young man, weren't you here when I told the class that Einstein himself had not been able to work this problem?"

That young man had not been told he couldn't solve the problem. The rest of the class hadn't even tried. Why should they try if Einstein couldn't solve the problem? But that young man had not heard those words of fear. He only knew if he solved the problem, he would get a better job. He needed the job, and he believed for the solution. Consequently, he got the solution to the problem. He later became dean of a mathematics school at a university.

Satan also stole from Job. He lost his purpose, position, possessions, family, health and money because of fear.

> The thing which I greatly feared is come upon me, and that which I was afraid of is come upon me.
> Job 3:25

The Bible says Job repented and God delivered him from his captivity (Job 42:6-10). Job ended up with twice as much in the end. He was again given seven sons and three daughters, and he saw his grandchildren to the fourth generation.

Job made a powerful statement when the test was over:

> If they obey and serve him, they shall spend their days in prosperity, and their years in pleasures. Job 36:11

Fear is perverted faith because it causes you to turn aside or away from what is good or true or morally right. Many people are highly developed in fear, which is a carnal force that comes from your spirit-man. But now you as a believer are getting your mind renewed and are becoming spiritually minded. You are discovering how to operate in the law of faith that lifts you up above the beggarly elements of this world.

Cowards Emphasize the Problem

A coward in our society is defined as one who fears and lacks courage to face and deal with a danger or problem or enemy. He is intimidated by his adversaries. That doesn't necessarily mean he is a coward in every area of his life.

However, fear attacks any and every area of life; and because of it, multitudes never make it into their promised land.

Satan was stealing from me. I had a problem that I would not deal with because the devil told me it could cause a church split. Since I was expecting the worse, I put the problem aside for a later day. The thief got in because I did not face the adversary when he needed to be faced.

Marte lost respect for me because I wouldn't handle the problem. I thought I was a big, bold, faith man; but then I looked at my life and saw several things I wanted to put on the back burner and not deal with. I learned fear was one of the doors allowing the enemy to get into my life and the ministry in particular.

I didn't want to deal with this particular problem because I was afraid of the results. I was expecting the worst instead of expecting the best. When I finally dealt with the problem, I caught the thief. Instead of the worst happening, the best happened. I made the thief restore what had been stolen.

Me? A coward bound by fear? Not me! But that's where the thief was getting in. I should have had my eyes on Jesus, and I should have expected the best. I should have said, "Lord, I will handle this for You. Our church will grow even more when this division and strife are stopped." Instead, I let it go; and the problem grew worse, almost causing an avalanche of problems.

When I saw the seriousness of the situation, I faced the problem, worked it out, and got Marte's respect back. She still loved me, but she didn't respect my behavior in that situation. She respects me now because I am not a coward. No woman respects a coward. She even tried to tell me so a few times, but I wouldn't listen.

When you fear, you worry. When you worry, you are meditating on the problem. When you meditate on the problem, you bring confusion and the inability to make a correct, quality decision.

I got to the place where I did not know what was right or wrong in that particular situation. I could not make the right decision because of the confusion.

When you are indecisive and procrastinate, you are feeding the giant of fear, instead of feeding your faith.

Faith cannot do anything for you until you get your eyes off temporal things and put them on Jesus and the Word. Until you get your eyes on the Author and the Finisher of your faith, you will be bound by fear.

Luke 17:5-11 says faith is the servant that works for you even while you are asleep. Feed him well with the Word of God, and he will do what you give him to do. Faith will act on what you believe to be true.

One of the major enemies of man is fear. Man acts and reacts to fear. When you find an area in which you are afraid, ask yourself, "Why am I afraid?" Look at what you are afraid of. See how fear got in. Then deal with it and get rid of it.

I straightened out the situation in our church, and it didn't split. It kept growing. It's amazing how easily we caught the thief.

> The fear of man bringeth a snare: but whoso putteth his trust in the Lord shall be safe.   Proverbs 29:25

Fear of what men think and fear of criticism bring a snare. Pastors cannot do what God wants them to do, if they are afraid of what men think about them.

Job was not safe because he feared, but whoever puts his trust in the Lord will be safe.

Conquer Fear—Enjoy the Fruit of Your Labor

One of the ten richest men in the world died a recluse at the top of a hotel in Acapulco. He died bound by a spirit of fear. I talked to some of the men who were there when he died and they said he was bound by mysophobia, the fear of germs, dirt and filth. Everything had to be spotless. He came out only at night when all the people left. He never got to enjoy life. However, when a man has his faith in God, he can be wealthy and enjoy it.

David killed the giant that was stopping God's people; but Goliath was not stopping them; it was fear. When you draw out of the faith of God, you can conquer fear and become a success in life.

> **He who conquers doubt and fear conquers failure.**

If a tree is firm, stable, and rooted in good soil, it will produce. If your life is firm, stable, and rooted in the correct things, why should you be afraid of problems? The only reason people are afraid is because they let fear rule them, instead of faith.

- Fear works against you, but faith works for you.
- Fear freezes God's best, and faith thaws it out.
- Fear expects the worst, and faith expects the best.

The Spirit of faith has come to give you life more abundantly.

The thief steals through your lack of knowledge. Now that you know more, don't let him steal from you. Do not trust in the things that you can see. Trust in the eternal things of God that you cannot see.

> Lay not up for yourselves treasures upon earth, where moth and rust doth corrupt, and where thieves break through and steal:
>
> But lay up for yourselves treasures in heaven, where neither moth nor rust doth corrupt, and where thieves do not break through nor steal:
>
> For where your treasure is, there will your heart be also.
>
> Matthew 6:19-21

4

Change Your Thinking

*As long as you trust your senses
and fear the problem, you
will never see the solution.*

Put your treasure, your trust, and your reliance in the things that are from above.
Don't lay up treasure on the earth in the carnal things you can see. If you trust only in visible things, the devil can attack you and steal them. But if you put your trust in the things you cannot see—the eternal things of God—the devil cannot steal from you, for God's power is greater than the devil's.

For years, Marte and I built our whole lives around what we could see, what we could hear, and what we could feel. We put our trust and our confidence in how things looked.

People buy stock that same way from the stock exchange. When they hear about some business declining, the stock goes down. When they hear about a business doing well, the stock goes up. The whole stock market goes up or down, usually because of fear of loss and greed.

Trusting in things you can see brings death. Moth and rust corrupt these things, and thieves break through and steal them.

Don't trust in your senses, for that is being carnally minded which is death. Instead, put your faith, trust, and confidence in being spiritually minded.

> For to be carnally minded is death; but to be spiritually minded is life and peace.   Romans 8:6

Think on the promises of God; there are over 7,000 of them, covering every area of life. To be spiritually minded you must know the promises of God's Word and set your affections on things that are above.

Fear enters through your mind. The thief gets to you through your ignorance of spiritual things that are not seen.

- Fear thinks on the *problem*.
- Faith thinks on the *solution*.

The problem exists, but faith knows it is better to think of the solution instead of the problem.

As long as you are thinking of the problem, you will never see the solution because you start fearing and worrying about it. Worry is meditating on the problem.

There are three days of the week when you should not fear, worry, think about, or meditate on a problem—yesterday, today, and tomorrow.

"You do not get ulcers from what you eat; you get ulcers from what is eating you" is a true old saying. You must put worry under your feet. Cast down those imaginations (II Corinthians 10:5). Don't trust in the things you can see in this life.

When you start meditating on the solution—God's promises—the way begins to clear. The Word becomes a lamp unto your path.

God makes a way where there seems to be no way. He will show you the way and will order your steps (Psalms 37:23). He will speak to you through the desires of your heart, through your conscience, and through your intuition. He will give you illumination, enlightenment, and direction.

Get your eyes on Jesus, the Author and Finisher of your faith. Get your eyes on the *Logos*, the Word. He will strengthen you and will show you the solution. He will give you that one inspired idea you need for your business. He will show you what God created you for. He is alive in you.

> **Word From the Lord for You**
>
> Oh, my little one who has been wounded and bruised by the enemy, I am come with healing and salve today to raise you back up. Fear came to steal, kill, and destroy. But I, Faith, have come to bring you life and to bring it to you more abundantly.

The only way your armor can be penetrated is when it is carnal and not spiritual. When you trust in the things you see, rather than the things you cannot see, the enemy takes advantage over you.

> When a strong man armed keepeth his palace, his goods are in peace:
>
> But when a stronger than he shall come upon him, and overcome him, he taketh from him all his armour wherein he trusted, and divideth his spoils.   Luke 11:21-22

Those whose armor is carnal and can be penetrated when the stronger one comes to spoil their goods are walking a broad way that leads to destruction. Those who walk that way are carnally minded and sense-ruled; they are concerned with how things look, how they feel, or what someone says.

The alternate way is narrow and has a narrow gate. Those on the narrow way wear a spiritual armor which keeps them spiritually minded, looking beyond the ordinary, looking beyond the problem.

When you wear the spiritual armor, you put your treasure in the things from above that you cannot see. Those are the things that no thief can break through and steal. There are few who choose the narrow way. You must decide whether you are going to be among them. You do so by being spiritually minded.

That which God created to work for you can work against you if you are ignorant of its existence and live in fear. All of us are designed to believe something; and we act on what we believe to be true, whether or not it is true. When you are motivated by the truth, it will produce positive results. When you are motivated by fear, Satan steals from you.

Let's Pray

Father, I submit and humble myself before You. I know it is not by might, nor by power, but it is by Your Spirit that we succeed. I know that no man can build Your house except You build it.

Every man builds things; but, Lord, You are the true Master Builder. Take my words and build Your house. Build Your people; add to them, precept upon precept, line upon line, here a little and there a little. Build up and release Jesus in their lives through the authority of the Name of Jesus. The anointing will break every yoke, the captives will be set free, and the thief—the devil—will be caught in every life. The door will be shut to him, and we will be strong. We praise You for it. In Jesus' Name. Amen and amen.

5

Examine the Thief's Origin

God created and commissioned man to rule the earth, not to be a servant to Satan.

The religionists have taught that you cannot expect much fulfillment in this life, but you can expect a whole lot of fulfillment in the life to come. However, the Word of God clearly disputes this.

> Godliness is profitable unto all things, having promise of the life that now is, and of that which is to come.
> I Timothy 4:8

> Nor trust in uncertain riches, but in the living God, who giveth us richly all things to enjoy.   I Timothy 6:17

God is for us much more than we have been taught. Did you know that God is a better employer than we let Him be? He will pay us better than we would ever pay ourselves. He delights in the prosperity of His servants (Psalms 35:27).

We must go back to the book of Genesis, where everything started.

> And God said, Let us make man in our image, after our likeness: and let them have dominion over the fish of the sea, and over the fowl of the air, and over the cattle, and over all the earth, and over every creeping thing that creepeth upon the earth.
>
> Genesis 1:26

Man was created in the image of God. He was created in paradise, in the middle of abundance; he did not lack any good thing. He was given dominion over circumstances; man had control.

The Scripture clearly states man was created, commissioned, and empowered by God to rule the earth.

> The heaven, even the heavens, are the Lord's: but the earth hath he given to the children of men.   Psalms 115:16

Although man was created with dominion, he was to fellowship and commune with God while he operated in this authority which he was given.

God told man not to eat of the tree of the knowledge of good and evil. When Adam disobeyed, he forfeited his dominion in the earth to Satan, his adversary, and man fell. The serpent deceived him, tricked him, and stole his birthright.

Man was to rule and to enjoy abundance; but he lost the abundance, together with his position in life.

Man was to exercise authority, dominion, control, and to govern the earth. He was to subdue and cultivate the earth so that it would produce fruit, but man lost his position.

Not only did Satan steal man's birthright, but he introduced fear, his most powerful weapon.

> And the eyes of them both were opened, and they knew that they were naked; and they sewed fig leaves together, and made themselves aprons...And he [Adam] said, I heard thy voice in the garden, and I was afraid, because I was naked; and I hid myself. Genesis 3:7-10

All the other creatures had fur, feathers, or hair; but man was clothed with the glory of God.

But the glow went out when he disobeyed God.

Some people read verse 10 and say, "Oh, they were nude." But there is more to this than just the physical. Man had been clothed from within with glory. When the disciples saw Jesus transfigured, his body was glorified; it was shining brightly (Matthew 17:2).

When man sinned, he was disrobed and disarmed. He lost his authority to rule and reign in the earth according to the promise of Genesis 1:26. He lost his glorious position with God. He lost dominion of the earth; he lost control (Genesis 3:14). Satan became the god of this world.

> Satan, who is the god of this evil world, has made him blind, unable to see the glorious light of the Gospel that is shining upon him, or to understand the amazing message we preach about the glory of Christ, who is God.
> II Corinthians 4:4 (TLB)

Man was to be the god of this world. He was not to be in servitude to the adversary. Man was to have control; but he became afraid when he knew he was naked.

"Naked" means *to be stripped of clothing, exposed, and without protection*. Man knew he was naked. He was stripped of his position, his armor, his power, and his authority. He was literally stripped and without protection or defense.

That is what happens when a soldier's patches, which show his rank and position, are ripped off. Man lost his honor and rank, and he fell into servitude to Satan, the adversary of God and man. Then Satan began to legally govern and control this earth, including taking dominion over man.

Man became afraid. A person who is afraid makes these statements. "I'm so worried. Everything I do turns out wrong. I just got over what happened to me the other day. I know better, but I just can't help it." These statements show loss of control.

The devil wants to keep you bound by fear, so he can keep you out of faith. He knows that if you get into faith, it will give reality to your life. It is faith that gives substance to [strength for] things hoped for (Hebrews 11:1). It is faith that takes you to God, because "he that cometh to God must believe that he is, and that he is a rewarder of them that diligently seek Him" (Hebrews 11:6).

Man had a position of power and control, but he lost his glory and his position; he was stripped of his rank and left defenseless. Therefore, God removed him from the Garden, and man who had been united with God was now alone.

Several years ago at the State Fair of Texas I saw a little girl crying because she had lost her parents. She was stricken by terror; fear gripped her little heart. She became confused and lost her direction; she didn't know which way to go.

Man was created to dwell and commune with God in the midst of abundance; but when that relationship was severed, God and man were separated. Alone, helpless, and defenseless, man was kicked out of the Garden of Eden.

God had said, "The day you disobey Me, you will die." Nevertheless, man transgressed and stepped out of faith [trusting God]. He sinned and was disconnected from God.

Man then became like a cut flower. When flowers are broken off the main plant, they look nice and pretty; but decay and death wither the flowers away because they are no longer connected to the source of life.

Fear, disobedience, and sin separated man from God when he sinned. Consequently, man was left alone, with no Lordship, no direction, and no authority.

6

Return to God, Legally

Jesus came to represent us, to make up for our wrongs, and to restore our rights which Satan had stolen from us.

Man had committed treason which is punishable by death. He had broken his promise, handed over control and authority to another, betrayed his loyalty, and given aid and support to the enemy. When man committed this treason, he was sentenced to die.

He could only be brought back to God through legal means, because everything God does is legal. So Jesus Christ became man's attorney, advocate, or intercessor to represent him before God the divine judge.

In order for man to be brought back into right relationship with God, the penalties for man's sins had to be paid for by someone, "for the wages of sin is death" (Romans 6:23).

> God is not mocked: for whatsoever a man soweth, that shall he also reap.
> Galatians 6:7

It amazes me that the same legal words used in the Word of God are used in law books and attorneys' speeches today. As our attorney, our legal counselor, and intercessor, Jesus Christ represents us, the plaintiffs, the ones with the complaints. He acts to obtain legal remedy for us.

A "remedy" is *a legal means of preventing or correcting a wrong or enforcing a right*; it is a means of recovering that which was lost through a wrong.

Jesus came to represent us and to obtain a legal remedy. He came to make up for the wrongs that we had done and to restore the rights that we had lost.

Therefore, He entered into a class action suit, which involves a group of people sharing the same grievance or loss of rights or possessions, before the divine jurisprudence. He identified Himself with us; and as our counselor, He went before the throne of God to obtain a legal remedy and to make up for our wrongs, so we could have our rights and possessions restored.

Judgment had already been pronounced. Therefore, there would have to be a repeal and what lawyers call "redress" in order for Him to go before the judge of the universe and once again plead our case. A "redress" means *setting right of what is wrong*. Jesus of Nazareth came to redress, to compensate for, our wrongs and to remove the cause of the grievance.

Several years ago Ralph Nader sued General Motors because of faulty gas tanks in some cars. His class action suit represented all of the automobile owners who had their rights or possessions lost because of the fault in these cars. He won the suit, and all of the people were sent letters informing them that the suit had been won and that General Motors was going to redress [make up for] the wrong. They would have their cars restored to a complete condition.

When Jesus won the class action suit, He Himself made up for our wrongs. When He was crucified and resurrected, He defeated the devil, spoiled principalities and paralyzed the enemy.

When Jesus had paid the penalties and redressed our wrongs, He obtained a remedy in His own blood; He purchased our freedom at Calvary. This class action suit is over, and man is free! That may not mean much to you, but it means a whole lot to God for He is the divine supreme court. If man was to come back to God, he had to come back legally. Man could be set free only after all the wrongs were made right. There had to be a remedy, and Jesus provided that remedy.

Right Of Redemption

When a suit has been won and the wrongs have been made right, then comes the right of redemption. You have a right to redeem that which was stolen, destroyed, or lost. Because Jesus purchased your freedom and made up for your wrongs, you now have a right to have your health, your position, and your rights restored. That condition is called righteousness, which is your legal right to abundant life. Claim it.

When you accept Christ, you are born again of the kingdom of God and set free from the curse of the law and the penalties of sin.

> There is therefore now no condemnation [judgment, condemned] to them which are in Christ Jesus, who walk not after the flesh, but after the Spirit.
> Romans 8:1

Deuteronomy 28, says fear and doubt are some of the curses that come because of disobedience. Galatians 3:13 says that Jesus delivered you from fear and doubt.

> Christ hath redeemed us from the curse of the law, being made a curse for us: for it is written, Cursed is every one that hangeth on a tree.
> Galatians 3:13

Our Advocate stood as a bridge between God and fallen man, who had been separated from God and who had no one to represent him, so that the wound could be closed. Jesus came to heal the bruise and to bring back total soundness by His stripes. The separation between God and man has been closed. Because of the blood of Jesus Christ and His atoning work at Calvary, you now have legal right to:

- Eternal life through Jesus Christ
- God's abundance
- Divine life
- Divine health

Calvary was more than Jesus just being wounded and bruised physically; it was a divine court case where justice was satisfied. Glory to God!

This may be new to you; therefore, you may need to read and study this a few times. However, it will build faith in your authority as a believer to know for a certainty that you have authority over the powers of darkness because you are no longer separated from God.

Your study of the Word of God progressively washes and purges you. John 15:3 says, "Now ye are clean through the word which I have spoken unto you." It did not say you are cleansed by trials and tribulations.

You are purged and cleansed by the Word. The Word develops and builds your faith so that you can stand your ground; the Word drives out doubt, unbelief, and fear. Fear came when man was left alone; but the love of God cast out all fear (I John 4:18).

The source of fear is being alone, without God. God says, "Do you want to be by yourself? I didn't create you that way. That's not the way your brain was designed to work. That's not the way your spirit was designed to work, and that's not the way this earth was designed to work. The earth was designed for you to move through Me and to exercise control throughout the earth."

When man sinned, he didn't die immediately; he began to wither away. But now that we have been restored, we are like trees planted by rivers of water which bring forth much fruit in season. Our leaves are not withering because our court case was redressed and a legal remedy was obtained. The remedy was Jesus identifying Himself as our substitute, so we could identify with Him.

The death He died was ours, not His. Because we are reunited with God through Him, we need no longer fear or be alone. Consequently, as we identify with His death, burial and resurrection, He seats us with Himself in heavenly places. Therefore, we must identify with His resurrection.

7

Find Your Position in Christ

When you know Christ has endowed you with power, rank, and authority, you need not fear any storm.

Jesus came to give us direction and to restore us to that original relationship mankind had with God—called sons of God.

> Beloved, now are we the sons of God, and it doeth not yet appear what we shall be: but we know that, when he shall appear, we shall be like him; for we shall see him as he is.
>
> I John 3:2

No longer are we naked; we have been clothed with the robe of righteousness. Once again we have been endowed with the power, rank, and position of a high level of authority. We have been given the ring of authority, as when the prodigal came home and the ring of authority was placed upon his finger.

No longer is our relationship broken. The wound has been healed; the separation between God and man has ended.

Isaiah 53 tells us that by His stripes He bought the remedy, the right of redemption, and redressed our wrongs. When He paid our penalty at Calvary, He brought us back into the presence of God. By His own blood He purchased our freedom.

You must now see yourself with Him. Close your eyes and envision yourself hanging at Calvary where Jesus hung in your place. You died with Christ; the old man that sinned was crucified with Christ. Not only is the old man dead, he is buried with Christ.

> Knowing this, that our old man is crucified with him, that the body of sin might be destroyed, that henceforth we should not serve sin.
>
> Romans 6:6

> Buried with him in baptism, wherein also ye are risen with him through the faith of the operation of God, who hath raised him from the dead.
>
> Colossians 2:12

> Therefore we are buried with him by baptism into death: that like as Christ was raised up from the dead by the glory of the Father, even so we also should walk in newness of life.
>
> Romans 6:4
>
> Even when we were dead in sins, hath quickened us together with Christ, (by grace ye are saved;)
>
> And hath raised us up together, and made us sit together in heavenly places in Christ Jesus.
>
> Ephesians 2:5-6

Glorified With Jesus

Now we are heirs of God and joint-heirs with Jesus Christ, and we have been glorified together with Jesus.

That word "glorified" means you have been *raised into a position of honor*. You were created in the image of God; now you have been restored to a position of power, authority, and sonship.

> The Spirit itself beareth witness with our spirit, that we are the children of God:
>
> And if children, then heirs; heirs of God, and joint-heirs with Christ; if so be that we suffer with him, that we may be also glorified together.
>
> Romans 8:16-17

When you are in Christ, old things will pass away. Have they passed away in your life? Has your old self passed away? Or are you still letting the thoughts of the old man rule you? You know you are a new creature in Christ Jesus.

> Therefore if any man be in Christ, he is a new creature: old things are passed away; behold, all things are become new. II Corinthians 5:17

Jesus bore the curse, so you could receive the blessings. He was rich; but for your sakes He became poor, so that you through His poverty could become abundantly supplied again.

> You know how full of love and kindness our Lord Jesus was: though he was so very rich, yet to help you he became so very poor, so that by being poor he could make you rich.
> II Corinthians 8:9 (TLB)

You are now in Jesus Christ. If you know who you are in Christ, and if you are planted by rivers of water, then you don't have reason to fear any storm.

Faith has come that we might have life. A portion of faith has been dealt to every one of us, so we can enjoy things like God enjoys them. Let your faith grow and began to produce for you!

> Through faith we understand that the worlds were framed by the Word of God, so that things which are seen were not made of things which do appear.
> Hebrews 11:3

We understand God has taken the foolish things of the world to confound the wise and the things that are not, to bring to naught the things that are (I Corinthians 1:28). We understand that Abraham received according to God's Word.

> Who against hope believed in hope, that he might become the father of many nations, according to that which was spoken, So shall thy seed be.
> Romans 4:18

The enemy knows that if you learn the principles of faith and conquer fear, you can change your world that he has ruined. That is why Satan doesn't like this faith teaching. He does everything he can to stop it because faith is the victory that overcometh the world.

8

Abide in His Love

Love drives out fear and is the perfect environment for full productivity and spiritual growth.

Although fears come because of your separation from God, they are driven out by love.

That Christ may dwell in your hearts by faith; that ye, being rooted and grounded in love,

May be able to comprehend with all saints what is the breadth, and length, and depth, and height; and to know the love of Christ, which passeth

> knowledge that ye might be filled with
> all the fullness of God.
>
>> Ephesians 3:17-18

A root is an organ of absorption. Therefore, being rooted in love gives you the ability to absorb [receive].

My wife Marte knows that I love her, and I know she loves me. Because of that love, she can receive from me. If she did not love me, we would be separated; and she would not receive what I have to say.

Likewise, because we are rooted in God's love, we can receive from Him. Because God is love, we receive love. The "root" of love gives you the ability to receive from God.

The word "grounded" means *an anchor or a support*. God loves you, and He is your anchor. Love is the foundation; it gives you the strength and the ability to receive from God. You love Him; you receive from Him. That love gives you the strength and the ability to receive from others, so love becomes the foundation of your Christian walk.

Belief Comes Out Of Love

Focus your attention and your faith on the love of God. God so loved you that He gave His only begotten Son, that whosoever believeth in Him should not perish but have everlasting life (John 3:16). Love is the foundation for belief. Marte loves me; therefore, she trusts and believes in me. Perfect love casts out fear.

> Faith...worketh by love.
>
> Galatians 5:6

Your faith works because it is established in God's love for you, which was demonstrated by Jesus at Calvary.

The word "belief" comes from the Latin word *lief* which means *beloved or precious, pleasing, agreeable, acceptable, willing, glad*. True belief comes out of that kind of love. That is why faith works by love. When you love someone, you believe in and trust that person. For example, Marte believes what I say; and she has faith to act accordingly. Faith is acting on what you trust to be true.

While man was connected to God, he had love, trust, and fellowship. But when man separated himself from God, he separated himself from love.

However, through Jesus Christ—the Gift of Love—man has been brought back to God.

> And to know the love of Christ, which passeth knowledge, that ye might be filled with all the fullness of God.
>
> Ephesians 3:19

> If ye abide in me, and my words abide in you, ye shall ask what ye will, and it shall be done unto you.
>
> John 15:7

Because Jesus is the Word and the manifestation of God in the flesh, and God is love (I John 4:8), we could read John 15:7 like this: "If you abide in Love." After you have been born again it is important that you not step out of love. You must guard your heart and not get into strife and fear, but walk in love. If you abide in Me—if you abide in love—you can ask what you will. If My words abide, you can ask what you will.

> And, lo, I am with you always, even unto the end of the world.
> Matthew 28:20

Love Is A Greenhouse

Several years ago, a friend of mine in Colorado showed me his greenhouse. Several inches of snow were on the ground outside, but inside the greenhouse were beautiful tomatoes and cucumbers, two to three times the normal size. He told me that the greenhouse had the correct atmosphere for the best growth of those plants, and that they were rooted in a special chemical which contained the correct diet of each plant.

A greenhouse is the perfect environment for the full productivity and growth of something. Love is a greenhouse. As long as you stay rooted and grounded in love, you are in the perfect environment for full productivity and spiritual growth.

You never want to step out of love, for outside of love is fear. Love gives you the foundation of belief and trust. Faith is acting on what you believe and trust to be true.

You need more than just a surface understanding of this subject; you need to *know* that your roots are planted in love. You are rooted and grounded in Christ, in love. You are in the greenhouse of love. Don't get out of it. If you do, you will freeze out there. You will be alone out there. But in love, in Christ, you can bring forth the ripest, most beautiful, and most plentiful fruit.

Word From the Lord for You

Beloved, don't be discouraged; don't be disturbed. I have not forsaken you. I have seen thy good works, and thy prayers have come up to Me. Yes, not prayers of doubt and unbelief, but prayers of faith.

Yes, saith the Lord, when you weep I weep. For when I see your tears, saith the Lord, I think about My love for you and how I only want you to understand that My love brings you supernatural miracle results. But you have to trust Me and trust My ways, for they are not your ways. They are not things that you can always understand.

But through your faith in My divine love for you, you can walk above the circumstances and know that I am working on your behalf to bring you the miracles that you need in thy life, saith the Lord.

Therefore, do not be discouraged, for when you are sad and discouraged, you nullify your faith and trust in My love for you. You stop My miracle provisions from flowing into thy life.

Look up and know that My love is providing for you even when you cannot see it, and let My joy be your strength. Let My peace be your comfort, and let My love build you up and keep you until your miracle arrives into your life, saith the Lord.

9

Be What God Created You To Be

You cannot do everything God created you to do until you are what He created you to be.

Your position in Christ establishes your position in life. You will never do anything big, bold, and brave without the confidence of knowing you are no longer alone because Jesus is Lord of your life.

Because Jesus is in you and you are in Him, He brings direction to your life, and you can say Jesus is Lord! Every time you say "Jesus is Lord," you are saying, "I now have direction."

When you really believe, and your belief is based on the love of God, and you hear His love letters to you [the Word of God], Jesus will be Lord of your life. Then because He is Lord in your life, you have direction.

Say it aloud right now: "I have direction. I am no longer lost."

Remember, fear came when man was separated from God; but you are no longer separated. Jesus brought you back and closed the wound. By His stripes you were healed (I Peter 2:24). You can now say:

> The Lord is my shepherd...yea, though I walk through the valley of the shadow of death, I will fear no evil: for thou art with me.
>
> Psalms 23:1, 4
>
> I will never leave thee, nor forsake thee. Hebrews 13:5
>
> Lo, I am with you always.
> Matthew 13:5

You are no longer separated from Him because the Lord is with you. Consequently, you will not fear whatever evil, problem, sickness, or disease comes knocking at your door.

Because Jesus made up for our wrongs legally, the penalties and injuries have been paid. We now have the right of redemption, which means we have legal rights to have everything that was lost in the Fall restored to us. Our rights include health, soundness of mind, prosperity, and being led by the Spirit of God.

When you need something, you must follow the scriptural laws and present your needs in words. Just as Abraham pleaded his case before God, you can plead yours through prayer (Genesis 19:20-33). There are several kinds of prayers you can use:

- Prayer of faith
- Prayer of agreement
- Intercessory prayer
- Prayer of binding and loosing

You are God's representative in the earth. Prayer is not just something that you can choose to do or not do. Prayer is a responsibility to plead your case and other people's cases before the throne of God. Knowing that your rights have been restored brings confidence. You will never attempt anything big unless you are confident someone big is with you. You can face a big world because you know Jesus as Lord is with you; then you have confidence.

When man is alone, he doesn't have the confidence to kill the giants. David said, "The God that was with me when I killed the lion is *still* with me" (I Samuel 17:37). David didn't kill that lion by himself. Nor did Daniel shut the lions' mouths in the den. God was with them and gave them confidence.

> Not by might, nor by power, but by my
> spirit, saith the Lord of hosts.
>> Zechariah 4:6

The Spirit of God gave Marte and me the vision to spread the Gospel to the four corners of the earth. Only God could give the energy, ability, and confidence to believe that this can happen. It is not our strength doing it; it is His strength.

God also gave you your vision, and He will provide the energy and ability for you to accomplish it.

In your fight against Satan and fear, Jesus Christ has also given you His power of attorney to bind things on earth so that they will be bound in heaven.

> Whatsoever thou shalt bind on earth
> shall be bound in heaven: and what-
> soever thou shalt loose on earth shall
> be loosed in heaven.
>> Matthew 16:19

Tommy, a recent leader of the Ku Klux Klan, was delivered from fear when he was saved. Here is his story of how he became what God created him to be.

"I had been in the hospital with a heart attack. Shortly after my release, I had to return because of a nervous breakdown. As I lay there thinking my world had come to an end, mental confusion, turmoil, and fear gripped me.

"Then I turned on the television, and there was Bob Tilton saying that fear, terror, torment, and fright came from Satan. He said Satan was a thief who had come to steal, kill and destroy; but Jesus Christ had come that we might have life, and that we might have it more abundantly.

"I made up my mind to find out more about that abundant life, because I didn't have it.

"I knew the power that fear had. I knew you can manipulate, intimidate, and control an individual's actions, even against their own free will, through fear. I had been influenced in the Ku Klux Klan by this Satanic propaganda. The devil had not come to talk to me visibly, but he controlled me by fear.

"I remember, I came to Word of Faith carrying my ceremonial hood and robe in a garbage bag. The church was very crowded so I sat three rows from the back, and fear and terror began to come back on me. Satan began to bring all he had against me.

" 'God', I said, 'I've done everything that You have told me to do. Did You send me over here to die?' I didn't say this out loud; I said it to myself, inside of my spirit. I said, 'God, You've got to help me right now. I'm dying!'

"Robert Tilton stopped preaching and said, 'You are just going to have to bear with me because I've got to be sensitive to the move of the Spirit.'

"He began to move about the congregation; this took several minutes. Finally, he came down the aisle to the very back where I was sitting, and he had a face of stone. He looked at me and smiled briefly. You have to remember that I thought he was going to throw me out, because he had a mean look on his face.

"When he smiled, I heard God speak to me. He said, 'I've heard your plea, my son.'

"Bob stuck out his hand to me and said, 'Do you believe?' He took me by the hand; and, instantly, I was set free from fourteen years of Satanic bondage.

"I had decided earlier that I was going to be an underground Christian. After everybody left, I was going to leave the bag with the preacher, confess my sin, and get out. I didn't know the Lord couldn't use underground Christians.

"I had told the Lord that He should take the bag. It was under my seat; so when Bob came to where I was sitting, I handed it to him. He threw it clear across the congregation toward the front of the church. Praise God, I was set free instantly!

"The next week, I sent a flaming summons to the members of the circle [Ku Klux Klan]. I denounced the Klan as a Satanic cult from the pits of hell. I told them that I denounced my membership and my oath. I told them that if any of them wanted to come with me and hear more of the truth to contact me. Three of them did, but not in the way I wanted to be contacted. They told me to take my family and get out of town, or out of the country, if I could. They had an emergency session of the inner council and had signed my death warrant with their blood.

"That came as no surprise to me. It was standard procedure for anyone in the inner circle who became a Judas to be terminated immediately for security reasons.

"What surprised me was that I was no longer bound by the negative Satanic force of fear. Now I walk in the positive power of faith. 'Greater is He that is in me than he that is in the world' (I John 4:4). 'If God be for us, who can be against us' (Romans 8:31)?

"I shared my testimony on the 700 Club with Ben Kinchlow and Pat Robertson. Ben was just the opposite of me; he was in the Black Muslims. In reality that is the Black Klan; we were opposites.

"He told everyone that had we met ten or twelve years ago—before our conversions—we would have been on opposite ends of automatic weapons, and one or both of us would have been dead. That illustrates the power of God to restore what was taken from you."

Tommy used to preach the gospel of fear; now he preaches the Gospel of faith, hope, and love. I am convinced Tommy is going to lead tens of thousands of people to Jesus Christ.

This truth of the abundant life in Jesus is a message that is going to resurrect the body of Christ to kill the giant of fear that has been defying the armies of God for several years.

The Davids are coming on the scene saying, "Is there not a purpose, is there not a cause, is there not a reason?" We are finding out who we are in Jesus. We are learning that our position in Christ releases our position in life.

The body of Christ is ready to:

- Blow out the doubt and unbelief
- Overcome fear
- Walk in the victory Jesus had given us through His blood at Calvary

You will never have what it takes to do, be, and have what God created for you until you realize that your position in Christ restores and releases your true position in life. In Christ, you are perfect, complete and righteous. So it is not what you *are*, but what you *think* you are that defeats you. In other words, when you think you are imperfect, incomplete and unrighteous, you are defeated.

> I can do all things through Christ which strengtheneth me.
> Philippians 4:13

You will never have the confidence to step out of the boat, as Peter did, until you know who you are in Jesus Christ. There is something special about Jesus. He knew Who He was; He knew He was the light of the world.

> Then spake Jesus unto them, saying, *I am the light of the world*: he that followeth me shall not walk in darkness, but shall have the light of life...Jesus answered and said unto them, though I bear record of myself, yet my record is true: *for I know whence I came, and whither I go*...And yet if I judge, my judgment is true: *for I am not alone*, but I and the Father that sent me.
>
> John 8:12,14,16

Here, then, are the steps to victory in your life:

- Learn who you are in Jesus Christ.
- Learn what you have because of who you are.
- Learn how to effectively use what you have because of who you are.
- Catch the thief that tries to steal your identity through fear.
- Shut the door on that lying devil.

You no longer have to be an outcast or walk in fear.

Let's Pray

Holy Ghost Power from on high, we believe You are present to break the yoke of bondage and fear.

You foul demon spirits of fear, you have worked against the body of Christ. You have held the body of Christians in bondage, but we have caught you. We have the Name of Jesus; we have our position in Him; and we know how to use the sword of the Spirit to overcome you. You have to leave. You have to flee. We resist you, Satan, in the Name of the Lord.

In Jesus' Name we pray. Amen.

A Word From the Lord for You

Many of you have become dry, thus saith the Lord, and stale in the things of God. I'm talking about faith, prosperity, and healing, but I am anointing you with fresh oil. I will not be outdone by the evil one. For when the enemy comes in like a flood, I will raise up a standard against him. For this is what I am doing in this hour.

A fresh anointing of My Spirit is sweeping across the land. It is coming out of My Word. For truly, you haven't seen anything yet of what I am going to do, but I shall reveal it to you by My Spirit.

Eyes have not seen, ears have not heard, neither hath it entered into the heart of man the things that I have prepared for them that love me. But by My Spirit, I am going to reveal them unto you, for it is given unto you to know the mysteries of My Kingdom.

So rejoice, for I will do a work in your life and in your day. Even if you saw it this very moment, you wouldn't believe what I am going to do through you. So don't give up! Don't throw in the towel!

Truly you will be anointed with fresh oil, and your voice will rise up, and your word will be as sweet as honey. Many shall come to you and shall stand around you just to listen to My wisdom that shall come out of your mouth, thus saith the Lord of Hosts.

10

Pursue Your Dreams

Fulfillment, the reward that brings excitement to your life, comes when you achieve what God called you to do.

We cannot *do* everything God created us to do, until we can *be* what God created us to be. We all want to be everything God created us to be, to do everything God created us to do, to have everything God created us to have. We want to possess our possessions and enjoy our inheritance in this life; that is our reason for being. If there is no reason for being, why be here? That is why so many people commit suicide.

> Yea, though I walk through the valley of the shadow of death, I will fear no evil: for thou art with me.
>
> Psalm 23:4

You are not alone. God is with you; and He says, "Go for it!" Step out of the boat. Run with the vision. Chart your course. See your dreams come to pass. Have success in life through Jesus Christ.

We are like trees. In the fall, when the weather gets cold, the sap stops flowing and the leaves dry up, wither, and fall off. But with the warmer weather in the spring, the sap begins to flow again. The leaves come out, and the trees blossom and bear fruit. The Holy Ghost, like the sap, is beginning to rise up, causing you to blossom and to bear much fruit.

Being Fulfilled

When you start achieving what God called you to do, it is called fulfillment. Fulfillment is the fruit and the reward of life; it brings excitement into your life.

I used to build houses. Every time I built a house, sold it, closed the loan, and moved some new people in, my heart would go pitter-pat. I felt so good. Achievement was the fulfillment, the fruit, and the reward of life.

Likewise, when you lead people to Jesus, you feel good, for you have birthed a baby into the kingdom of God. The reward of life is to eat and enjoy the fruit of your labors. There is a problem, though. Very few people are fulfilled. Not everyone enjoys the fruit of their labors. Not everyone knows what it is to bite into a sweet Washington apple, or a ripe Elberta peach from Georgia, or corn on the cob from Texas.

The devil has stolen the strength and the faith of people who are unfulfilled. Fear grips them, and they are bound and miserable.

Unfulfilled people are discouraged, disgruntled, discontented, miserable, and dissatisfied. They resent those who are happy and fulfilled; and that brings envy, restlessness, complaining, faultfinding, murmuring, and griping. Unfulfilled people, most of the time, will blame their unfulfillment on those who are fulfilled.

"Unfulfill" means *not bringing to realization, not carrying out or developing to the full potential, not achieving, not accomplishing, not completing*.

Not doing what God created you to do brings you unfulfillment.

> Where there is no vision, the people perish. Proverbs 29:18

When people are fulfilled, they are happy. They also want everyone else to be blessed.

One couple in our church started out earning $600 per month; now they are making more than $5,000 per month. They recently shared with me that they had thought more people would be excited about the Word working in their lives; but, instead, they caught flack and persecution because of their success.

So if you intend to prosper, you will have to pay the price to continue loving people, whether or not they understand what is happening in your life.

A healthy plant grows and produces fruit. Likewise, if you are growing as a person, you are a happy, fulfilled, achieving individual. Man was created to bear fruit and to enjoy fulfillment. Deuteronomy 30 says we are free moral agents, and we have the power of choice.

God said He has set before you life and death, blessing or cursing, and you should choose life, that you should live.

> But the word is very nigh unto thee, in thy mouth, and in thy heart, that thou mayest do it.
>
> I have set before you life and death, blessing and cursing; therefore choose life, that both thou and thy seed may live.
>
> Deuteronomy 30:14,19

I think many people are sick physically because they have gone through their entire lives without seeing any of their dreams accomplished. When dreams don't come to pass, discouragement follows.

Hope deferred maketh the heart sick
Proverbs 13:12

Keep thy heart with all diligence; for out of it are [flow] the issues of life.
Proverbs 4:23

But we have caught the thief! Now we have confidence and we can do all things through Christ Jesus.

A Vision Is Like Your Goal

It is very important for you to know your major purpose in life. Otherwise, you are like a ship going to sea without a compass. You have no direction, no purpose, and no goal in life. The enemy causes you to fear and lose confidence, then he steals your vision.

As soon as Peter got enough faith to get out of the boat, the devil sent storms and boisterous winds to challenge his faith. Then Peter got his eyes off Jesus, the Author and Finisher of his faith, the One Who would complete his vision. When Peter looked at the problems, the "What ifs," and the "What are we going to do nows" around him, he began to lose confidence and to sink.

As long as Peter looked to Jesus, he drew strength; but when he got his eyes off Jesus, off his vision, and off his major purpose in life, he began to sink. At that same point, you, too, will begin to sink and become disoriented, unfulfilled, and resentful toward those who are fulfilled.

Get your eyes off other people and other churches. Stop comparing yourself with other people; just compare yourself with Jesus. Let Him tell you what He has called you to do, and you will become happier and happier each day.

Without a vision, the people perish. The devil has been stealing many people's visions and dreams, and they wonder why they are unfulfilled. They wonder why they have murmuring, strife, with sickness and disease in their bodies. They are miserable, and they want everyone around them to be miserable also.

Get your eyes back on what God called you to do, and it will put wind back into your sails. Then, when you see something come to pass, you will become excited, encouraged, and energized.

God wants you to believe He is a big God Who will never leave you alone. Oral Roberts has been through many problems: family deaths, persecution, books maligning him, lack of funds; but he has pursued his dream. Each time, God has brought him through victorious. One of the things I respect most about Brother Roberts is that he doesn't give up.

Because God brings others to success, you know He'll do it for you. So stop licking your sores, and encourage yourself in the Lord. Pursue your dreams! You will not fail. You will recover all the things Satan has stolen from you, and you will possess all your possessions.

Amanda's Miracle

A little girl named Amanda had a remarkable healing and miracle because of her mother's faith in God.

Amanda was born with Kartagener's Syndrome, a severe disease that affects the lungs. It had caused her to have pneumonia 27 times by the time she was two years old! This, in turn, caused bronchiectasis, which deteriorated her lungs.

Amanda had no sinus cavities, her heart was on the wrong side, and her organs were displaced. Because she didn't get enough oxygen in her brain, they had to put her on an oxygen machine or she would go into grand mal seizures.

Every day Amanda's mother had to use two machines on her just to keep one lung going. (The other lung had no air in it for over a year!) One of these machines, the nebulizer, had to be used on Amanda three times a day to force mist into her lungs to help the mucous come up.

Each morning, Amanda's mother had to clap or beat on her little girl's back, chest, and sides to get the mucous coughed up. Amanda would cry because she had become so sore from the daily beating. Can you imagine being a mother and having to hit your baby on the back and make her cry every day just to get one lung going? It was horrible!

One Sunday Amanda's uncle and his family invited Amanda's family to my church, Word of Faith. I called for people with lung and chest problems to come forward for me to lay hands on and pray over them in the Name of Jesus.

Amanda's mother had heard that I was going to pray for the sick in Jesus' Name and lay hands upon people to ask Jesus to heal them. Amanda's mother heard the truth that Jesus is the same today as He was yesterday (Hebrews 13:8).

She believed that God could heal her daughter. So she brought her daughter to our miracle service. There, she saw all kinds of people being healed and receiving miracles in their bodies. In this service, Jesus healed people's bodies—the blind, the maimed, the crippled, the insane—just like He did almost 2,000 years ago!

When I laid my hands on Amanda and prayed over her, Jesus healed her! Amanda told me that before I prayed her lungs had been clogged up, but Jesus had just made it so she could breathe.

Three weeks later, Amanda had a checkup and her mother said the doctor reported that there was air in Amanda's left lung for the first time in over a year! Her mother told the doctor Amanda was no longer on any medication and didn't have to use the machines; and she didn't have to beat Amanda anymore either.

The doctor asked what they had been doing to get her healed, and Amanda said, "Well, Jesus healed me!"

The skeptical doctor couldn't deny that Amanda was healed, but he didn't know how. He told them to just keep doing whatever it was that they had done.

Amanda's mother had turned to God out of desperation. She had tried everything else.

God honors faith. When we love Him and know how much He loves us, faith works. Faith works by love because it is rooted and grounded in love (Galatians 5:6; Ephesians 3:17).

Being rooted gives us the ability to receive, because roots are organs of absorption. Being grounded means our foundation for belief is trusting God. You are in Jesus, and He has provided everything you need. God is so great, yet people limit Him.

> Yea, they turned back and tempted God, and limited the Holy One of Israel. Psalm 78:41

God says your unbelief has hindered you from receiving His love. You must put "success in life" principles to work in your life, so God will be glorified when you bring forth fruit. Then when you pursue your dream, the power and the glory of God will break the yoke of fear and discouragement.

Let's Pray

I rebuke discouragement and the foul demon spirits of fear. I come against you is the Name of Jesus Christ of Nazareth. You have held people in bondage. I break you off them in Jesus' Name, and I command you to loose them. I command you to come out of them. I command you to set them free. Set them free!

Right now the Holy Spirit flows into you, my beloved brother or sister. The power of God flows into your body, breaking the yoke of sickness and disease. The power of God flows into you to break and replace every yoke of bondage with His blessings. Healing virtue flows through you, in Jesus' Name.

11

Establish Your Goals

Big visions must be chopped into little parts and enjoyed a piece at a time.

God directs you through the godly desires of your heart. Your hope is your dream, your vision, or the desire of your heart.

Many people set unrealistic goals; and when they cannot be met, they become discouraged and lose their vision. Their hope is deferred [or postponed], and it makes their hearts sick.

> Hope deferred maketh the heart sick: but when the desire cometh, it is a tree of life.   Proverbs 13:12

However, when something that you desire comes to pass, you get excited and full of energy.

Sometimes we have such big visions we never chop them up into little parts and enjoy them a piece at a time.

I have learned that you can cause more desires to come to pass by using a bit of common sense.

- Determine your vision
- Set long range goals
- Set short range goals
- Release your faith daily for some accomplishment

"When the dream cometh, it is a tree of life," so that you can enjoy fulfillment of achievement. When a dream comes, you get strength; and that keeps you going.

Since I've learned this, each morning I pray and come up with one or two things that I can accomplish that day. If I accomplish four or five things in a day, I'm so proud of myself because I saw a few of my dreams come to pass.

> Which HOPE we have as an anchor of the soul, both sure and stedfast, and which entereth into that within the veil. Hebrews 6:19

It is important to keep your vision before you and not lose it. Your heart's desire is like a seed; if you water it and act upon it, it is the starting point of all achievement and fulfillment. Desire acted upon is power.

When you begin to act upon your dreams and visions, you will be amazed at the energy that will begin to flow through you to see those dreams become reality. Dreams have what it takes to give you the energy to see them through. Through faith, God framed His world; and through the act of faith, you can frame your world.

When we started to enlarge the church and build our new learning center, I got all fired up on what I called "Ten Thousand in '82!" I would preach and stir everybody up, including myself, and say, "Next Sunday, we're going to double. Everyone bring one. Boy, what are we going to do? Where are we going to put them all?"

The next Sunday would come, and it looked like we had fewer than the Sunday before. I became very disappointed. We did not see "Ten Thousand in '82"; nor did we see ten thousand in '83.

I tried to stir everybody up to win a soul to Jesus. We had Soul Winning Sunday, Holy Ghost Sunday and Miracle Sunday. Then my secretary said, "Bob, last Sunday morning people called from nearly every state in America, receiving the baptism of the Holy Ghost." That was on Holy Ghost Sunday.

The next Sunday was Healing Sunday, and we had miracles happening all over the place. A cripple was healed in Puerto Rico when he laid his hand on the television set. In prayer I said, "Come out! Come out! Come out, in Jesus' Name!" The man wrote me a letter and said, "My leg popped out on the third "Come out!"

These things were happening nationwide; we really had surpassed our goal of 10,000 because we had begun broadcasting our services live by satellite. But I felt like no one wanted to reach our local community. Consequently, I got really discouraged and felt rejected.

I climbed into bed, covered my head with the pillow, opened my Bible and licked my sores. I was overcome, so I had a little pity party. I had a little overcoming situation to deal with.

I sense there are some pastors reading this book who are very discouraged about the size of their church. They have worked their hearts out to build that church and to help you believers get fed, but they're getting discouraged.

Some people think, "Bob has this big church; he never goes through anything like that. However, they don't know that the bigger the church, the more you must use the Word.

So I lay in bed, licking my sores. Turn with me to I Samuel 30, and I will show you where I was. I had heard David had a tough time, so I said, "Ah...I'll read about David."

David and his men had been helping the Philistines fight against some enemies. Then the Philistines told David to give them a hug and go home; they didn't need David any longer. Similarly, the world says, "We don't need you. Good-bye shepherds, pastors, preachers, and church people; we don't need you any more."

> And it came to pass when David and his men were come to Ziklag on the third day, that the Amalekites had invaded the south... and smitten Ziklag, and burned it with fire.
>
> And had taken the women captives, that were therein: they slew not any, either great or small, but carried them away, and went on their way.
>
> So David and his men came to the city, and, behold, it was burned with fire; and their wives, and their sons, and their daughters, were taken captives.
>
> Then David and the people that were with him lifted up their voice and wept, until they had no more power to weep. I Samuel 30:1-4

When I had read that far, I said, "I could relate to that." Not only did I feel like the church had deserted me—they hadn't—but I felt like Marte didn't understand me. She couldn't imagine my doing this "Ten Thousand in '82" thing. I felt like the whole world had deserted me.

> And David's two wives were taken captives, Ahinoam the Jezreelitess, and Abigail the wife of Nabal the Carmelite.
>
> And David was greatly distressed; for the people spake of stoning him...
> I Samuel 30:5-6

As I recall, I had just received some hate mail; somebody didn't like something I said somewhere. Believe me, I get my share! Now, here are David's own men turning on him. He's getting more alone by the minute; things are not getting better, they are getting worst. Not only had his family been taken from him, but now his very own men turned against him. These were the men who did great exploits of faith with David.

> David was greatly distressed for people spake of stoning him...

I went, "Um...They wanted to kill him."

> ...because the soul of all the people was grieved, every man for his sons and for his daughters: but David encouraged himself in the Lord his God.
> I Samuel 30:6

There was no one to encourage me, so I began to encourage myself, too; and I read on.

> And David said to Abiathar the priest, Ahimelech's son, I pray thee, bring me hither the ephod. And Abiathar brought thither the ephod to David.
>
> And David inquired at the Lord, saying, Shall I pursue after this troop? Shall I overtake them. And He answered him, Pursue: for thou shalt surly overtake them, and without fail recover all. I Samuel 30:7-8

This is when, literally, the Word of God ignited like fire in my spirit-man. There I was licking my sores. I felt sorry for myself, rejected, and like no one really cared. We had an awesome responsibility; there were bills everywhere, and we were endeavoring to reach humanity with the best-kept secret in the world.

The Lord told David, "Pursue: for thou shalt surely overtake them, and without fail; you shall recover all." Then David went out after what he had lost.

- **PURSUE**—Go for it!
- **OVERTAKE**—Overcome!
- **WITHOUT FAIL**—Succeed; have good success in life!

I read that and said, "WOW!" This is what built up in my spirit: PURSUE YOUR DREAMS! If the devil has stolen your vision and has gotten your eyes off of what God called you to do, if you feel rejected and no one cares, and everyone has left you, God says to you this night: "PURSUE YOUR DREAMS!"

Follow after your dreams. Set your course for your star. Go on with it; don't stop. Don't let the devil [the thief] use fear or discouragement to steal your vision and purpose in life.

Don't let him take the wind out of your sails. Set yourself some little goals, so that you can enjoy their fruit every now and then. Don't set your dreams by other men's visions; set your dreams by what you can do now, and feast on that accomplishment daily, weekly, monthly, and yearly. Get your eyes off of everybody else and what they're doing; get your eyes back on Jesus.

Cheryl Prewitt dreamed of being Miss America. Then she was in an automobile accident, and her life was goofed up. One leg was shorter than the other, and she limped. But she had a dream, and she kept pursuing it. She didn't give up.

> For a dream cometh through the multitude of business.
>
> Ecclesiastes 5:3

> But the hand of the diligent [honest, energetic, organized, consistent applied effort] maketh rich.
>
> Proverbs 10:4

Many times she went through pageants and lost. Although she didn't win, the dream was still there; so she kept going. She didn't let the devil discourage her, nor did she lose her heart. She kept going.

When I read God's instructions to David, the Lord said to me, "Bob, you'll overtake [catch up with and go beyond]."

> For there is no restraint to the Lord to save by many or by few.
>
> I Samuel 14:6

In other words, God doesn't know any limits. You'll overtake without fail; you will recover all.

Not long ago, I went to see R. G. LeTourneau's place in Longview, Texas. This is now one of the largest manufacturers of heavy earthmoving equipment in the world.

This man had a dream. God gave him an inspired idea of a special plow blade, and he ended up building a multi-million dollar heavy equipment company. We saw the first little trailer that moved a bit of dirt; then we saw the other massive machinery, plants, factories, and warehouses. Finally, we saw a college that he funded out of his private profits. LeTourneau poured millions of dollars into the Gospel, and God returned it to him hundredfold.

Henry Ford envisioned the first mass-produced automobile. Never had that been done before, and he became the father of mass production.

He wanted to build an eight cylinder engine, and his engineers told him it couldn't be done. He kept sending them back to the drawing board because he was pursuing his dream. Finally, they came back with the V-8 engine which revolutionized the automobile industry.

A run-down amusement park inspired Walt Disney to build a nice, clean park where families could enjoy a weekend of relaxation and being together. He was a man who spent time with his kids and his family. He dreamed of building the first theme park. Although it had never been done before, he pursued his dream.

Many times as he created Mickey Mouse, the Mickey Mouse Club, his movies and television series, he had severe financial problems which would have caused some people to give up. But he did not give up! He kept pursuing his dream. He didn't let the flame go out. He kept at it.

Most of us give up too easily. We've been little pansies or big babies.

But God has given us the sword of the Spirit, His Word. He is saying to you, "Pursue your dream. You'll overtake, and you will recover all!"

Leonardo da Vinci was a great artist, engineer, musician, and scientist who lived in the late 1400s. He sketched the first helicopter, but it was never built.

ESTABLISH YOUR GOALS

Approximately 400 years later, a minister's two sons manufactured bicycles in Kitty Hawk, North Carolina. They believed that man could fly, and that they could build a flying machine with a gasoline engine. No one had ever done that before, but they pursued their dream.

People said, "Man can't fly."

They would say, "Man can fly." They had a dream, and they pursued it.

Then on a grassy knoll in Kitty Hawk, on December 17, 1903, one of the brothers got into a flying device. History was made as the flying machine took off and went approximately 200 feet in about 60 seconds. History was made because they refused to give up! Now jets screech across the sky, traveling at speeds greater than sound.

> Many shall run to and fro, and knowledge shall be increased.
>
> Daniel 12:4

Henry Ford, Walt Disney, Wilber and Orville Wright, and Cheryl Prewitt believed in their dreams. They established goals and kept on going; they didn't stop.

In one of the worst moments of my life the Lord said, "**Pursue**."

I said, "Lord, you don't understand. Nobody cares, including my wife."

He said, "**Pursue! You'll overtake, and without fail you shall recover all; because the Lord knows no restraint.**"

Without fail means you will succeed. You will overcome every adversity and every obstacle; you will remove every mountain and pluck up every sycamore tree, if you will not give up. You will succeed because you are not alone.

> I will never leave thee, nor forsake thee.
> Hebrews 13:5

> Lo, I am with you always, even unto the end of the world.
> Matthew 28:20

> Yea, though I walk through the valley of the shadow of death, I will fear no evil: for thou [the Lord] art WITH me.
> Psalms 23:4

We've caught the thief that has been crippling humanity. It is not God's will for 20 per cent of the people to have 80 per cent of the money. God wants you to be rich and abundantly supplied; He wants you to live in divine health and see your dreams become reality, as you seek first the kingdom of God. He said that when you seek Him first, the things the world seeks after will be added to you.

> If ye be willing and obedient, ye shall eat the good of the land.
> Isaiah 1:19

No good thing will he withhold from them that walk uprightly.

Psalms 84:11

Let the Lord be magnified, which hath pleasure in the prosperity of his servant. Psalms 35:27

Beloved, I wish above all things that thou mayest prosper and be in health, even as thy soul prospereth.

III John 2

Bring ye all the tithes [and offerings] into the storehouse, that there may be meat in mine house, and prove me now herewith, saith the Lord of hosts, if I will not open you the windows of heaven, and pour you out a blessing, that there shall not be room enough to receive it. Malachi 3:10

12

Regain Your Possessions

You can demand your rights and make the devil restore what he has stolen from you.

If a thief be caught...*If.* He may not be caught everywhere he is stealing; but *if he be caught,* he has to restore to you what was stolen.

To "restore" means *to replace or give back something which was lost*. It also means *to put back in a prior position*, such as restoring a king to office. It means *to bring back to health, to bring back into being or existence*. The thief must restore or bring back.

> I will restore to you the years that the locust hath eaten, the cankerworm, and the caterpillar, and the palmerworm, my great army which I sent among you. Joel 2:25

God said He will restore the years that the enemy has destroyed. So let's learn about regaining your possessions, and making the thief restore to you everything that belongs to you. After all, God created you to have those possessions; and the Word of God declares you are an heir of God and a joint-heir with Jesus.

When you are born again, you are transformed. You experience a metamorphosis; you are no longer a worm, you become a butterfly. You are transformed by the renewing of your mind (Romans 12:2). Therefore, you can change your thinking about yourself, and see your world changed.

You have received a revelation of Christ in you, the hope of glory (Colossians 1:27). Paul had the same revelation when he said, "Christ liveth in me."

> I am crucified with Christ: nevertheless I live; yet not I, but *Christ liveth in me*: and the life which I now live in the flesh I live by the faith of the Son of God, who loved me, and gave himself for me. Galatians 2:20

> I can do all things through Christ
> which strengtheneth me.
>
> Philippians 4:1

I am not talking about what *you* can do. I am talking about what Jesus Christ can do in and through you. Through Him you can do all things. When you invited Him to live in your heart, you discovered it was the King of kings and the Lord of lords Who came inside your heart. Not some little weakling, but Jesus Christ the Son of God came to live inside you. This is your position in Christ.

> If ye abide in me, and my words abide
> in you, ye shall ask what ye will, and
> it shall be done unto you.
>
> John 15:7

Jesus didn't put any limits on this promise. If ye abide in Him, and His Words abide in you, you can ask what you will, and it will be done for you. That is Bible. It might not be your doctrine, but it is the Bible.

This kind of faith causes the sick to be healed and the dead to be raised. Blind eyes see and deaf ears hear when you believe Jesus lives on the inside of you. At the moment you believe, you have the family name, the ring, and the robe of authority put back upon you.

Get out of religious thinking. Abandon traditions which have robbed the Word of God of its power. Jesus said you have nullified the Word of God because of your traditions.

> Thus you nullify the word of God by your tradition that you have handed down. And you do many things like that.
> Mark 7:13 (NIV)

The miraculous should be commonplace in every church. Every church that is called of God ought to have crutches, braces, and other discarded medical aids all over the walls, as we have at Word of Faith World Outreach Center. That is the kind of church Jesus wanted us to build!

> Is it not written, My house shall be called of all nations the house of prayer?
> Mark 11:17

He wasn't talking about saying, "Lord, if it be thy will." He was talking about coming against the powers of darkness and shaking the powers of the devil. He was talking about demanding your rights and making the devil restore what he stole from man in the fall! Restoration means getting back what belongs to you.

Some people say, "Well, I can't handle all of that."

Are you saved? What did you get saved from? Paul said, "I am not ashamed!"

> For I am not ashamed of the gospel of Christ: for it is the power of God unto salvation to every one that believeth; to the Jew first, and also to the Greek.
> Romans 10:8

> He therefore that ministereth to you
> the Spirit, and worketh miracles
> among you, doeth he it by the works
> of the law, or by the hearing of faith?
> Galatians 3:5

If the power of God is not present, miracles will not happen. If a minister preaches that Jesus doesn't perform miracles anymore, then miracles won't happen in his church. But when you preach that Jesus is the same today as yesterday, and believe it, then you will see that His acts are the same.

> Jesus Christ the same yesterday, and today, and forever.   Hebrews 13:8

Let Jesus really be Lord in your life today. Then you won't be concerned with man's works that win you a Sunday School pin or pennant. Instead, you'll be wondering how many people got saved, received the baptism of the Holy Ghost, were healed, and how many devils were cast out.

If you are called Christian, then you had better be like Christ. That is what the word Christian means.

Some people say, "I'm a Catholic;" "I'm a Baptist;" "I'm a Methodist."

We should all say, "I'm a Christian."

If you are a Catholic first and foremost, you will act like a Catholic. If you are a Baptist first and foremost, you will act like a Baptist. But if you are a Christian first and foremost, you will act like Christ.

It doesn't matter what the sign on the front of your church says; if you like good Word teaching and are born again and live like it, you are a Christian. You will live like Christ.

Many people want to improve their circumstances, but they don't want to pay the price to improve themselves. Don't be that way! Eagerly pay the price!

> Beloved, I wish above all things that thou mayest prosper and be in health, even as thy soul prospereth.
>
> 3 John 2

Even as *your soul* prospers. It didn't say as the pastor's soul prospers. It didn't say as Jesus' soul prospers. It says as *your soul prospers*, you can be in health. As you prosper in your soul, your mind will be renewed to what is truth.

13

Refuse Limitations

You don't have to be confined to the world you are in now; you can break out into a brand new, bigger world.

A farmer once went out into his pumpkin field and looked down the rows of little baby pumpkins, just popping open and beginning to form. He took a gallon jar and stuck a little pumpkin in it.

Fall soon came, and all the pumpkins grew bigger and bigger. One day he looked at the gallon jar. All the pumpkins were bigger than the one in the jar. That little pumpkin had filled up the jar, but that was as big as it grew.

Like the farmer, you set your own boundaries and limitations, relative to what you have believed for. Jesus said, "According to your faith be it unto you" (Matthew 9:29).

If your believing is little, then your receiving will be little. If your believing is big, then your receiving will be big. In other words, the size of your faith determines the size of your world. David said the Israelites limited the Holy One of Israel because they wouldn't believe Him for big things.

> Yea, they turned back and tempted God, and limited the Holy One of Israel. Psalms 78:41

The Chinese used to tightly wrap cloth around the feet of little girls to keep their feet small. They called it foot-binding. Just because of the wrapping, those little feet wouldn't grow very big.

After Jesus raised Lazarus from the grave, Lazarus was alive; but the people had to get the grave clothes off him. If he had kept those grave clothes on, he wouldn't have gone anywhere. Likewise, the renewing of your mind unwraps the grave clothes off you.

Many people are alive, but they are bound like mummies. When it is time to raise their hands and praise the Lord, as Psalms 134 instructs us to do, some people just can't seem to get their hands up. Their hands seem bound to their body.

However, when you are free, you can raise your hands and say, "Thank You for forgiving me of my sins! Thank You, Lord, for healing my sick body!"

By doing this, you are unwrapping the grave clothes off yourself. You are freeing Christ within you, the hope of glory.

Just as certain goldfish won't grow any larger than their bowl or pond allows them to grow, so you set your own limitations.

Your thinking has limited you because you have conformed to this world, like that pumpkin to the jar. You thought that what you do inside that jar is the limit of how far you can go, and you can't get out. That is as far as your life can go until you renew your mind to all God has for you.

> Be not conformed to this world: but be ye transformed by the renewing of your mind, that ye may prove what is that good, and acceptable, and perfect will of God. Romans 12:2

- **Don't be conformed to sickness!** Renew your mind. Find out that health is available.

- **Don't be conformed to poverty!** Renew your mind. Find out that prosperity is available.

- **Don't be conformed to fear!** Be transformed by the renewing of your mind. Find out that God has not given us a spirit of fear, but of power, and of love, and of a sound mind (II Timothy 1:7).

- **Don't be conformed to this world!** Get your eyes off its limitations.

Set your affections on the things above, where the Holy One of Israel lives. Set your affections on the One Who knows no limit or restraint. Set your affections on the One Who said He is with us always.

In Texas we love barbecue. There are contests in Dallas and around Texas to see who cooks the best barbecue. The news media checks all over to see who has the best barbecue ribs.

A man in our church recently decided he wanted a barbecue restaurant. He already had a fish restaurant, but he wanted to add a barbecue restaurant. He looked in the newspapers, but he couldn't find any for sale.

The world depends on the newspapers; and many people become hopeless when they can't find what they are looking for in the papers. But we have taught the people at our church to find a need and fill it. If there isn't a job, make a job. All jobs exist to fill a need. There is still plenty of need, so there are still plenty of jobs. You have to get your eyes off the newspapers, and stop listening to the news; you must start listening to the Holy Spirit.

This man said, "If there isn't a barbecue restaurant for sale, I'll just build my own." He couldn't find a location, but he didn't let that stop him.

He got an inspired idea, because God knows no limits. This man wasn't living in a gallon jar. He didn't have his brain wrapped in grave clothes. He had gotten his mind renewed, and he knew there was no limit with God.

This man bought a pickup truck and a trailer and remodeled it into a portable barbecue store which he parked on a street corner where there were no restaurants. He parked his trailer with the barbecue sign on the top, and that aroma began to fill the air. He got the aroma blowing in the right direction and crossing that busy traffic—and guess what?

He soon had two trailers; then three; then four. I believe he has about eight of these barbecue trailers on corners now.

I drove past one the other day. Mmmm, that hickory smoked barbecue smelled so good!

You see, he didn't let what he saw limit him. He had his mind renewed to the bigger One living on the inside of him.

Have you ever heard of a Flea Circus? Fleas can be trained. They are put in a container with a glass lid on top. Those little fleas jump up and hit their heads on the glass lid. After about a week of jumping up and hitting their heads on the lid, they stop jumping up that far. They stop about a quarter of an inch from the top. After a while, the fleas are trained. You can take the lid off the container, and the fleas will not jump out. They are limited because of what they think.

Some years ago there was a man who decided to do something great with his life. His name is John Goddard. I first learned of him when I read his life story in the *Reader's Digest* (October, 1983).

This man followed God's principles of having a vision, planning, then carrying out that plan with persistence and patience.

In 1940, when John Goddard was fifteen years old, he saw people around him doing just about nothing. He wrote a list of 127 things he wanted to do during his life.

Here is the list of what he wanted to do. He wanted to explore these rivers: the Nile, Amazon, Congo, Colorado, Yangtze, Niger, Orinoco in Venezuela, Rio Coco in Nicaragua.

He wanted to study primitive cultures in the Congo, New Guinea, Brazil, Borneo, Sudan, Australia, Kenya, the Philippines, Ethiopia, Nigeria, and Alaska.

He wanted to climb Mount Everest, Kilimanjaro, McKinley, Kenya, Fuji, the Grand Tetons, and others.

He wanted to photograph Victoria Falls, Sutherland Falls, Yosemite Falls, and Niagara Falls.

He wanted to explore underwater coral reefs in Florida, the great Barrier Reefs in Australia, the Red Sea, Fiji Islands, and the Bahamas.

He wanted to explore the Okefenokee swamps and the Everglades. (These were his first achievements.)

He wanted to visit the North and the South Poles, the Great Wall of China, the Panama and Suez canals, Easter Island, Vatican City, the Taj Mahal, the Eiffel Tower, the Blue Grotto, the Tower of London.

He wanted to swim in Lake Victoria and Lake Superior.

He wanted to become an Eagle Scout, dive in a submarine, land and take off from an aircraft carrier, fly in a blimp, a balloon, a glider, ride an elephant, a camel, an ostrich, and a bronco.

He wanted to skindive to forty feet, hold his breath two and a half minutes underwater, catch a ten-pound lobster.

He wanted to go to church.

He wanted to follow the John Muir trail.

He wanted to study native medicines and bring back useful ones.

He wanted to bag camera trophies of elephant, lion, rhino, cheetah, cape buffalo, and whale.

He wanted to learn to fence, teach a college course, watch a cremation ceremony, explore the depths of the sea, appear in a Tarzan movie.

He wanted to own a horse, a chimpanzee, a cheetah, and an ocelot.

He wanted to build a telescope, write a book, publish an article in National Geographic, high jump five feet, broad jump fifteen feet, run a mile in fifteen minutes, weigh 175 pounds, perform two hundred situps and twenty pullups.

He wanted to learn French, Spanish, and Arabic, read the entire Encyclopedia Britannica, read the Bible from cover to cover, read the works of Shakespeare, Plato, Aristotle, Dickens, Thoreau, Hemingway, Twain, and others, become familiar with compositions of Bach and Beethoven.

He wanted to become proficient in the use of an airplane, a motorcycle, tractor, surfboard, rifle, pistol, canoe, microscope, football, basketball, bow and arrow, lariat and boomerang.

He wanted to compose music, watch people walking on fire, milk a poisonous snake, shoot a match with a .22 rifle bullet and light it, become a member of the Explorers Club and the Adventurers Club, learn to play polo, travel through the Grand Canyon on foot and in a boat, go around the globe four times.

He wanted to visit the moon someday, if God wills.

He wanted to marry and have children. (He has five children now.)

He wanted to live to see the 21st century. (He will be 75 when the 21st century comes.)

This young man decided his life was not going to be mediocre and boring. He was going to look beyond the normal. He was going to do things in his life. I never found out how long it took him to figure out what he was going to do.

In 1977, John Goddard was 53 years old, and 103 goals of his original list of 127 were completed. In 1977 he had earned approximately $50,000 speaking about his adventures. By 1983, at age 59, he had completed 106 of those goals.

How much more can be done through believers who will just step out of the boat and let God do what He wants to do in their lives!

Basically, humanity sits in the boat and complains about the others who got out. Let's all get out of the boat.

I am endeavoring to unwrap your brain and get your eyes open to the resurrection power of Jesus Christ that is inside you. This is more than being delivered from hell after death.

If that was all there was to it, that would be more than enough to cause me to make Jesus

Christ Lord of my life. But there is more than getting delivered from death after death. ''This is the victory that overcometh the world, even our faith'' (I John 5:4). We can be delivered from the hell that is in this life.

14

Expect a Sevenfold Return

When you believe God's Word more than you believe your feelings or circumstances, you can expect a sevenfold return.

This blessing started with Abraham in Genesis 22. It is a perpetual promise that God made to Abraham, and Christ extended to Gentiles who believed on Him.

> That in blessing I will bless thee, and in multiplying I will multiply thy seed as the stars of heaven, and as the sand which is upon the sea shore; and thy seed shall possess the gate of his enemies;

> And in thy seed shall all the nations of the earth be blessed; because thou has obeyed My voice.
>
> Genesis 22:17-18

> Christ hath redeemed us from the curse of the law, being made a curse for us: for it is written, Cursed is every one that hangeth on a tree:
>
> That the blessing of Abraham might come on the Gentiles through Jesus Christ; that we might receive the promise of the Spirit through faith.
>
> Galatians 3:13-14

I read the Bible several times without seeing this. *Christ has already redeemed us from the curse*; that means He has already purchased our freedom and made restitution for our wrongs. He has already restored us from the curse of sin. He has already caught the thief!

God made a promise to Abraham: "In blessing I will bless thee, and in multiplying I will multiply thy seed." You must believe it is the will of God for you to prosper and be in health.

Some say prosperity is not God's will for this life; but if that were true, then why did Jesus go about doing good and healing all that were oppressed of the devil?

> God anointed Jesus of Nazareth with the Holy Ghost and with power: who went about doing good, and healing

> all that were oppressed of the devil;
> for God was with him.
>
> Acts 10:38

Why was the Son of God manifested? That He might destroy the works of the devil.

> He that committeth sin is of the devil; for the devil sinneth from the beginning. For this purpose the Son of God was manifested, that he might destroy the works of the devil.
>
> I John 3:8

Jesus healed the sick and prospered humanity. He prospered both Peter in his fishing business and the little lad with the five loaves and two fishes. He had authority over nature and over supply and demand.

You must realize that:

- By Him and through Him were all things brought into existence.
- You are in Him, and He is in you.
- Your position in Jesus Christ releases your position in life.
- It is the will of God for you to prosper and be in health even as your soul prospers.

When your soul prospers, your eyes will be opened to God's abundance. Did you get that? God's Word opens your eyes.

- If you can't see a job, God gives you the faith to create a job.
- If you can't see money, God will give you the faith to create money.

You won't think there aren't any barbecue stands for you; you will know there is one waiting for you. You will find that you do not have to see one. You have the faith of God; and with that faith, you can create one. It is God who gives you power to get wealth.

> Remember the Lord thy God: for it is he that giveth thee power to get wealth.
>
> Deuteronomy 8:18

Second Kings tells about Elisha, who had a double portion anointing. Jesus said, regarding those who believe, "The works that I do shall he do also; and greater works than these shall he do" (John 14:12). As a result of Elisha's anointing, abundance came to the widow who was broke.

Next there was a woman who didn't have any children; but the anointing through the prophet of God gave the woman a child. The child died, but out of death came life.

> Then spake Elisha unto the woman, whose son he had restored to life, saying, Arise and go thou and thine household, and sojourn wheresoever thou canst sojourn: for the Lord hath called for a famine; and it shall also come up on the land seven years.

> And the woman arose, and did after the saying of the man of God: and she went with her household, and sojourned in the land of the Philistines seven years.
>
> And it came to pass at the seven years' end, that the woman returned out of the land of the Philistines: and she went forth to cry unto the king for her house and for her land.
>
> And the king talked with Gehazi the servant of the man of God, saying, Tell me, I pray thee, all the great things that Elisha hath done.
>
> And it came to pass, as he was telling the king how he had restored a dead body to life, that, behold, the woman, whose son he had restored to life, cried to the king for her house and for her land. And Gehazi said, My lord, O king, this is the woman and this is her son, who Elisha restored to life. II Kings 8:1-5

After seven years' absence, she found somebody had taken her house and land. So she went to the king and told him she wanted her house, her land, and whatever belonged to her restored.

This was the same woman who talked the man of God into prophesying her a child. Then when the boy died, she talked the prophet of

God into leaving what he was doing to go raise him back to life. This little woman knew how faith worked.

- She knew the God Who had given her the child.
- She knew the God Who had raised her child from the dead.
- She knew the *same* God, and that same prophet of God, would make the king restore her house and land.

She wasn't going to let the thief steal from her any longer. He had to restore sevenfold. She went to that king and told him she wanted what belonged to her restored to her.

> And when the king asked the woman, she told him. So the king appointed unto her a certain officer, saying, Restore all that was hers, and all the fruits of the field since the day that she left that land, even until now.
>
> II Kings 8:6

That was seven years worth! She believed God, and she exercised her authority. It is amazing, but it works! When you get out of doubt and unbelief and start acting like this little woman, then you will get some things from God.

Sometimes God requires that you move forward without any visible sign from Him. When God told Joshua to take the children of Israel into the promised land, He told him to cross over

Jordan, but the waters did not part. The people didn't see dry ground when they got up that morning. The Bible says the waters parted only when their feet touched the water (Joshua 3:13-17).

God always expects you to face your problems. The city of Samaria was surrounded by the enemy; no food was getting in and no one was getting out. There was famine, lack, poverty, sickness, and disease inside the city. The enemy, the devil, had stopped them from going out into what belonged to them. (II Kings 7:1-11).

Four lepers who sat outside the camp said, "Why sit we here until we die?" If they went back into the city, they would die. If they stayed there, they would die. If they went forward, they just might live. They got up and walked toward the enemy. They began to go toward their problem. They didn't let the enemy cause them to fear.

The Bible says that when they began to go forward, God caused the enemy to hear a great noise of chariots and armies and men. When they heard this, the enemy fled, leaving everything behind.

The four lepers walked into the enemy's camp, and everything they needed was there—food, clothing, and supplies.

When they went back to the starving city and told them what had happened, the city didn't believe them. The lepers told them there were food, prosperity, soundness of mind and healing for their bodies out there, but the people sat in their "religious" camp and would not believe them.

If you don't believe, what are you going to do with all the crutches and braces hanging on the wall of our church which were left by people who were healed?

What are you going to do with the whole Bible? What are you going to do with the verse that says, "Jesus Christ the same yesterday, and today, and for ever" (Hebrews 13:8)?

What Bible are you going to read from? If you remove all the miraculous power from the Bible, there won't be any pages left; and there won't be anything to read.

As you read the Bible, you find that God is a miracle-working God Who has always been *for* man. So much so that He gave His Son, Jesus Christ, as a cure for sin.

The Bible says the lepers finally convinced the people of Samaria to get up and go look. Nothing happened until those four lepers decided to do something. Nothing happened until they decided to change their thinking and go forward.

John Goddard decided to accomplish those 127 goals. He decided not to sit there and let his life rot away, doing nothing. He wanted to live life to the fullest.

You can do big things! God created you to do them. These principles will work for you, but you must renew your mind and believe them.

It isn't any big deal for God to prosper you. He just doesn't want you to be greedy; He wants you to be liberal. A liberal soul is made fat (Proverbs 11:25). In our church, the ones who have been liberal over a period of years are the ones God has prospered and blessed.

If you don't believe in prosperity, forget it; you are not ever going to prosper! If you don't believe in healing, forget it; you are not ever going to get healed.

God's blessings come though faith. They come through believing or trusting God's Word more than you believe how you feel and more than you believe circumstances.

The town of Samaria looked doomed because it was shut off by the enemy, but those four lepers didn't care what it looked like. They got up, went forward and acted like what it could be. When the men from the town started toward the enemy's camp, they found the enemy had discarded their clothing, weapons, jewelry—all their belongings—along the road.

The Word of God says when you get up, dust yourself off, and start going forward, the enemy will flee before you seven different ways (Deuteronomy 28:25).

God likes sevens. God told the Israelites to march around Jericho seven days. He promised that the thief must restore what he stole from you sevenfold. Revelation speaks of seven candlesticks, seven churches, seven seals, seven angels. Naaman, bound by leprosy, dipped seven times in the river Jordan. When the prophet Elisha raised the woman's son from the dead, the Bible says he sneezed seven times.

In Joshua 6:1-5, God told Joshua, "I want you to march around the walls of Jericho once a day for seven days. On the seventh day, I want you to march around it seven times. When you have marched around it seven times on the seventh day, I want you to blow the trumpets and SHOUT!"

That was the shout of faith. The Israelites did what the man of God said because they respected the anointing on the prophet of God. Those walls of Jericho fell down. Similarly, the walls in your life will fall, if you will believe.

The Word of God daily changes people's lives. Let's look at one more testimony of the healing power of God.

"My mother suffered for six years with pain in her chest, face, and down one arm. We had taken her to seventeen or eighteen different doctors and to three hospitals. She had surgery on her neck, but the pain got worse. She was taking eleven pain pills and six to eight muscle relaxers a day, but none seemed to relieve the pain.

"I had been watching Robert Tilton's daily television program; and I just knew that if I could get my mother to watch, she would be healed," said her daughter. "So I told her about the program."

"I thought, I've tried everything else, and it didn't help," said the woman. "Well, I got busy with something else and forgot about it.

"One day my daughter just popped in. She asked, 'Mamma, may I listen to my program?'

"I said, 'Why certainly, honey.'

"She turned on the television and said, 'This is Daystar (the previous name of Success-N-Life program).'

"I began to listen to it and to get drawn up into it. I felt better just watching.

"Then I called for prayer, and God healed me!

"Back in 1934, an automobile hit me and crippled my left leg. The accident had left it one inch shorter than the other.

"When I called for prayer, I didn't even say anything about this leg, but that night my left leg was just as long as my right leg. I could walk without holding on to tables or chairs, or leaning against the wall. I could get up out of bed and do things.

"God has changed my life so much. Now, I can look around and see that we are all humans who need God; I needed Him a lot."

This woman has simple, childlike faith. Isn't that a beautiful story?

Satan has used fear, man's number one enemy, against each of us. The thief [fear] cometh not, but for to steal, and to kill, and to destroy; but Jesus [the Word, the *Logos*], has come that you might have life, and have it more abundantly (John 10:10). Faith comes by hearing the Word (Romans 10:17). Faith has come that you might have life, health, and eternal redemption—to restore to you what the thief stole from you in the Fall. For he hath made him to be sin for us, who knew no sin; that we might be made the righteousness of God in him (II Corinthians 5:21).

Several years ago, I meditated on this Scripture day and night. One night the reality of *being the righteousness of God in Christ* literally got down in my spirit. I learned I am no longer a filthy rag, no longer a nothing I have been re-created in Christ Jesus into something beautiful. That experience almost took my breath away.

Then, in a vision, I found myself standing in the presence of God; He was right behind me. Before me was a mass of humanity as far as I could see. Each of them was bound, afflicted, and tormented with diseases. It was a most hideous sight. As far as I could see was hurting, hurting, hurting humanity.

I heard Jesus say, "Many of my ministers pray *for* my people, but I want you to *pray the prayer of agreement*."

I remember saying to myself, "I've got to remember this."

The presence of God was so strong. I knew He was right behind me, about fifty feet away, above my head. I didn't see Him, but I heard Him say, "I want you to pray for them."

> If any two of you shall agree on earth as touching any thing that they shall ask, it shall be done for them of my Father which is in heaven.
>
> For where two or three are gathered together in my name, there am I in the midst of them.
> Matthew 18:19-20

You and I are gathered together in the Name of Jesus right now. Make your decision! Decree and declare what you want God to do in your life. Take your step of faith today, and I will agree with you for your miracle. There is a well of blessings and creativity that is ready to spring up within you, so start charting your course by the dreams in your heart.

Plant your seed by the faith that is in your heart, and it will immediately start to grow. Success will follow you as you follow God and pursue your dreams.

15

Act Upon God's Word

Step into that dimension of faith where God lives, where there is always peace, love, blessings, and prosperity.

Satan started robbing Roberta of her most precious possessions when she was a little girl. First, he stole her parents and family.

She was raised by her half-sister's Christian grandmother who taught her to know the Lord, but she did not experience the love of her own family as a little girl needs.

Years later, after Roberta had married, the thief tried to steal her family again. Her husband,

Mike, used drugs and alcohol. Although she knew this was not pleasing to God, she went along with his lifestyle to please him.

Despite all Roberta did to keep her husband, she still lost him. In 1983, he was arrested, convicted of dealing drugs, and sentenced to two years imprisonment.

During those two years, Roberta came back to God and started feeling her self-worth. One day she watched our satellite seminar at her church and was instantly healed of back pain caused from a pelvis that had been crushed in a car wreck nine years earlier.

Even though she had come to know Jesus Christ, Roberta backslid when her husband was released from prison. Mike soon began drinking and taking drugs again.

Two years passed and Roberta found herself needing to support the family, since Mike was funneling most of his money into drugs and alcohol.

Then one morning Roberta happened to find our program on television. During the program, she realized she was leaving God out of her life. So she repented and made a $1,000 vow of faith to show God she was serious.

Later, after Roberta explained the principle of vowing to Mike, he also called in a $1,000 vow of faith for his salvation and for deliverance from drugs and alcohol.

You don't buy salvation. They were worshipping God through their giving a thanksgiving offering in the form of a vow.

A few hours after Roberta sent her first check towards the vow, she received a good job. Encouraged by this blessing, Roberta expected God to do more for them.

Today both Mike and Roberta are saved. Roberta has received the baptism in the Holy Spirit and is delivered from fear and depression. Mike has been delivered from his bondage to drugs and alcohol.

Roberta's family has been restored. Mike, Roberta, and their children read the Bible together daily; and they stand together as a family—for God and against Satan—claiming all the joy, peace and happiness that was stolen from them for so long.

In a flash, Florence's world went up in flames. All her possessions lay scorched or in the ashes of what once was her home. She and her two children were left without shelter.

Florence's situation intensified her despair. Her unhappiness vented itself in verbal abuse of her children. Strife dominated the family, and Florence continually fought with those around her.

Florence battled alcoholism and depression; she spent years listening attentively in Alcoholics

Anonymous. She learned about God, but she never accepted Jesus Christ as her personal Savior.

One day Florence happened to turn on the television and saw our program. Something clicked in Florence's heart when she heard me say, "I can help you."

Florence desperately wanted help. She needed deliverance from the bondage that had stolen her joy, peace, and happiness. She wanted God operating in her life, but felt she was too bad to ever be forgiven.

That day, Florence called our prayer line. The phone minister told her she could come to God as she was and become a new creature in Jesus Christ, so Florence accepted Jesus as her personal Savior.

Since she lived nearby, the phone minister invited her to attend our church services. Florence cautiously entered the sanctuary, not knowing what to expect; but her fellow Christians welcomed her with such love that Florence immediately felt right at home. Later Florence received the baptism of the Holy Spirit.

Since then, Florence has learned about making and paying vows of faith to God, and calling upon Him in times of trouble. On one occasion Florence needed a car. Since she had made vows to God, she felt she had the right to expect Him to help her get one. Shortly after this, one of her friends bought her a used car.

Since she had lost everything in the fire, Florence also needed a refrigerator and living room furniture. Another friend gladly gave her these items.

The more Florence trusted God and let go of her finances by giving to the ministry, the more God restored things in her life.

Today Florence is actively involved in Bible study, home fellowship, and ministering to others. God has restored the joy, peace, and assurance the thief had stolen from her.

A thin blanket covered the exposed, hard, rickety bedsprings where Wanda and her two-year-old daughter sometimes slept. Separated from her husband and expecting another baby, Wanda had moved into her aunt's already overcrowded house.

Since her aunt's children and their families also occupied the house, it was often difficult to find a place to sleep or something to eat. Wanda often went hungry.

Wanda's baby was born crippled and undernourished. The malnutrition was due to Wanda's insufficient diet.

Wanda prayed for years for God to heal her son's disability; but when no miraculous cure came, Wanda accepted her son's awkward walk and stopped praying. His condition became "normal" to her—not a concern to bring again before the Lord.

Although Wanda had given up hope for her son's healing, Jesus was waiting for her to demonstrate her faith in Him. One day Wanda watched our program and made a $1,000 vow of faith to God. Later, she received an anointed red prayer cloth from us.

She passed the prayer cloth between her children who both had bad colds. At the time, although Wanda thought only of God's relieving her children's cold symptoms, her faith was released.

Before long Wanda noticed something different about her son's walk. Then she realized his feet were straight and normal. God has restored what Satan had stolen from her son so many years before.

Entrenched in the drug scene, Larry lived his life in states of drug-induced highs or wanton drunkenness. His irresponsible behavior angered his mother.

One day he came home to find that she had sold his car to pay debts he owed her. In anger, she exiled him from her home. Larry's actions had apparently "killed" the love she once held for him.

Larry reestablished himself, though it was difficult without transportation. Then one day he happened to watch our television program. As he heard the anointed Word of God, his faith grew; and he decided to call our prayer line. He prayed the prayer of faith with a phone minister and made a $500 vow of faith to God.

Today Larry's life has miraculously changed. He has been delivered from drugs and alcohol, and he associates with Christian friends.

Shortly after Larry's rebirth, he started looking for a car. For four months, he searched, but he was not able to get financing on any car he found.

Then Larry spied a 1984 Volkswagen Rabbit which was in excellent condition. Not only did he get a good price on the car, but his mother co-signed for the financing.

Satan had controlled Larry through drugs and alcohol, but Jesus set him free. The enemy stole his mother's love, but Jesus rebuked the devourer and restored that love sevenfold, all because Larry released his faith in a miracle-working, loving God.

Nancy and Danny had moved from one state to another searching for a job. God had blessed them with one, but it was seasonal.

After seeing me on television, Nancy decided to call the prayer line and make a vow to God. A few days later Danny received an offer of a permanent job in the state from which they had moved. The job was with a well-known telephone company, and they decided to go for it.

The position was his, but there was no money to help them relocate. They applied for a loan through the credit union where Nancy had been a member for four years; but because they had no collateral, their application was turned down. The company which had hired Danny could not help them because he was going in at an entry level. Nancy, however, had made a vow to God that He would bless them in ways they had not expected.

Danny's father had not been at all pleased when Danny and Nancy had married, and he had really not said much to Danny in six years; in fact, he had not even met Nancy. Danny had been very hurt by this situation and he longed to be at peace with his father, so he decided to go see him. During his visit, Danny's relationship with his father was restored, and his father loaned them the money they would need until Danny's first paycheck. Nancy and Danny feel this was a real miracle.

Although their finances are still somewhat limited, they look forward to a pay raise and full benefits through Danny's company in six months. As grateful as they are about their job and the restored relationship with Danny's father, they are more joyful about their faith in the God Who supplies their every need.

16

Catch the Thief

When you give to God, He rebukes Satan and breaks the thief's power against you.

God wants you to make it in life. He wants to bless you even in the midst of all the turmoil and problems that you may be going through. He has divine plans for your prosperity, even when there seems to be no way and no hope.

Many today have lost their dreams and their hope of ever making it because of the great problems that our country is facing—problems that no man can solve on his own.

Many people offer strategies and solutions to help our ailing nation. However, while we need natural plans, these are not the only answers to solving the problems of people that are hurting and sick, or don't have jobs, or don't have the money to pay their bills.

We are not limited by NATURAL answers! Faith is rising up in me; I know in my spirit that there are SUPERNATURAL answers to these problems. Then I heard the Lord speak to me and say:

A Word From the Lord for You

This whole nation is cursed because they have robbed Me. But if they will prove Me now, and begin to worship Me through their tithes (10%) and their offerings, then I will heal this nation.

For truly, saith the Lord, as the people go, so goes the nation. If this nation and the people of this nation—if My people—will humble themselves and once again put Me in first place in life, no nation will be able to stand before them all the days of their lives. For I want to bless this country. Yea, I want to bless all countries.

So this very day, saith the Lord, I am anointing thy life with an inspiration and a revelation from Me. Speak to My people.

Challenge this country to prove Me and to put Me first and watch Me open the windows of heaven unto her, and unto all those that will put Me first, saith the Lord.

For I will turn this nation around; I will turn individual lives around. And for you that will honor Me and worship Me, yes, and prove Me even this very day, saith the Lord, I will begin to do a work in your life that has not been before.

For this nation had known Me. But moral decay began to come in and My people's love for Me began to wax cold. But, yea, saith the Lord, I am raising up a new standard. And those that begin to put Me first even as in the days of old, I will cause the Philistines and their enemies to envy them because I will bless them, saith the Lord, even as I did Isaac in time of famine.

So teach them, saith the Lord, and instruct them, exhort them, encourage them to put Me first and to prove Me. And I will open the windows of heaven and I will pour them out blessings, saith the Lord, that there is not room enough to receive them all. And I will rebuke the devourer for your sakes and He shall not destroy the fruits of your ground. And neither shall

> your Gross National Product be eaten up, saith the Lord, by the aliens. For truly in this day and in this hour I will have a people, if they will trust Me.
>
> I have placed a blessing upon this Word, saith the Lord. Yea, this Word is conditional. And for all those that believe it and act upon it—for those that are doers of it and not hearers only— surely the anointing, the inspiration, the divine direction, and the receiving from Me will come forth into their lives. And they shall grow up to be as the tree planted by the rivers of water, whose leaf does not wither, saith the Lord, who brings forth fruit in her season.
>
> So prove Me now, saith the Lord. And yea, you've hungered for the Word from Me. You have sought Me and you've asked Me to help you, saith the Lord. Rise up and act upon this fresh anointing. And it will bring a quickening to thy spirit-man and will open thy eyes and give thee light for thy path this day. For this is your Word that you have sought Me for, saith the Lord.

You see, there is a special blessing and anointing upon this Word. It's fresh. It's alive. It's from the throne and the heart of God. I want you right now to prove God, just like He said.

Obey this Word; don't be a hearer only.

Malachi 3:8-12 says that when you rob God of tithes and offerings, you are cursed. When you withhold your tithes and offerings which are His rightful share of our wealth, you place yourself at risk. Then Satan [the thief] can attack you. However, if you have not robbed God, you can catch the thief, and God promises to rebuke him for your sake and break his power against you.

When you give in faith, you are going to receive in faith. If you give to a ministry that isn't doing anything for God, it's like throwing your money away. God is not pleased with that. I believe that you need to give where you see God moving. This ministry is teaching people how to give, believing they will receive from God. As you give, you are storing up blessings in Heaven, then when you need something you can withdraw from your heavenly bank account.

If you are tithing and giving in faith and are living a holy life, then all you need to do is to ask the Father boldly for whatever you want—marriage, house, business partnership, whatever the devil has stolen from you.

If you haven't been tithing, then you don't have the right to demand those things. What you need to do is to rely on God's love, His mercy and compassion. Then give Him your best gift to show your faith.

I want you to step into faith. I want you to step into that dimension where God lives, where there is no lack, nor fear, nor sickness, nor turmoil. Step into that dimension where there is always peace, love, blessings, and prosperity. I want you to take a step of faith and prove God with your tithes and offerings today—not tomorrow—but today. RIGHT NOW!

I challenge you in the Name of Jesus to send $100 right now. Somehow, someway do whatever you have to do to get this $100. Maybe you can send more; maybe you can't send quite that much. But I challenge you right now to step into faith and do everything that you can do to step into this dimension of faith.

Because when you give from your heart and it takes faith, you step into God. You step into God's best and into His miraculous provisions for you.

This is it! This is one of the most powerful revelations and one of the most anointed prophecies that God has ever spoken to me. This is your day to prove God for your miracle. I don't care how big it is or how small it is. Whatever miracle you need, I believe God said for you to prove Him.

When God says to prove Him, it's time to prove Him. I challenge you to prove Him now with a $100 offering. Seed into the work of God and help us carry this Elijah-anointed ministry to the four corners of the earth.

> ### A Word From the Lord for You
>
> Yea, saith the Lord, and those that bless you, I will bless them. For I have raised you up to take My Word to the four corners of the earth. Yea, I have raised you up to take My Word to those that have never heard of My Word before.
>
> For My love is everlasting, saith the Lord. And I love the uttermost as much as I love you. But I have touched you and anointed you, and those that bless you I will bless them, saith the Lord, not only with material blessings and answers to their needs and prayers, but they will also be storing up riches in heaven where rust and moth cannot corrupt and thieves do not break forth and steal, saith the Lord.
>
> For I will use you and I will use them, saith the Lord to be My arms, to be My mouth, to reach out to those that have had no one reach out to them. So tell them again, saith the Lord, to prove Me this day and see Me move in their lives and open up My windows of heaven unto them and rebuke the devourer that's been destroying their lives, saith the Lord.

My friend, you are not buying my prayers. My prayers are free. Jesus said, "Freely ye have received, freely give'' (Matthew 10:8). God has given His supernatural power and anointing to me, not for myself, but for me to minister to you. That is why I give of myself and pledge to pour out my heart in prayer for you.

When you give, you are not buying from God. You are worshipping Him through your giving, which shows Him that He is your Source—not you. You don't buy God's blessings; but the Bible does say worship Him with sacrificial gifts.

All through the Bible, men and women consistently worshipped God through giving offerings and sacrificial gifts. God always manifested Himself in their lives, and He will do the same for you when you worship Him with sacrificial offerings. David said he would not give God that which cost him nothing (II Samuel 24:24). Many times people want all of God's blessings, but they won't release their faith and worship Him through their giving.

Giving is not the only way to release your faith, but it is one of the more powerful ways. By giving, you are saying with your actions, ''God, I put You and Your kingdom first. As I help You with Your business, as I pour out my soul into the lives of others, I believe You are going to help me to see my dreams become reality.''

This is the key to your miracle: Obey the Lord quickly. There's no time to waste. Send your best gift of $100 or more today and write me your most urgent prayer needs on the prayer page included at the back of this book.

The presence of God is very strong right now. He wants you to prove Him today. It's important to move while the Spirit of God is moving, so don't delay. Mail your prayer needs and your best gift of $100 or more to prove Him today for your miracle!

My dear friend, before you lay this book aside, make sure you put God first so you too may have the desires of your heart.

First, ask Jesus to cleanse you of your sins. You don't have to clean up your life first—God will do it for you. He will also give you a new heart, new desires, and the Spirit of truth.

If you follow these new desires—which are based on God's Word—you will have a beautiful new life on Earth, and eternal life.

Pray this prayer out loud and believe:

"Father in Heaven, I've heard Your Word, and I want to be born again. Jesus, cleanse me of my sins. I want to be a child of God. I want to give my life to You. Make me a new person. Be my Lord and Savior.

"I believe I'm now born again, because the Word of God says I am! Jesus is my Lord. Thank You, Jesus, for a new life. Amen."

Now, don't go by what you think or feel. Go by what God's Word says. You are saved—you are born again. Believe it!

If you prayed this prayer sincerely, then call us at our 24-hour prayer line—(214) 620-6200—and a prayer-minister will help you. Or, write for more information (with no obligation):
"Salvation Information"
Robert Tilton Ministries
P. O. Box 819000 • Dallas, Texas 75381

ROBERT TILTON MINISTRIES
Miracle Pledge/Vow Covenant

...Pay thy vows unto the most high and call upon me in the day of trouble; I will deliver thee... **Psalms 50:14**

☐ I'm acting on this anointed word. Here's my "Prove-God Offering." $ _____
TF-4125-500

☐ Enclosed is my offering toward my previous pledge/vow to help you in God's work. $ _____
TF-4125-500

☐ I'm making a New "Seed of Faith Vow" of $_____.
OSNL
Enclosed is my offering of: $ _____
TF-4125-500

☐ Enclosed are my tithes to the work of God. I believe God will rebuke the devourer and open the windows of Heaven into my life. $ _____
AA-4125-100

Upon the first day of the week let every one of you lay by him in store, as God has prospered him (I Cor. 16:2).

TOTAL $ _____

CAT

RETURN THIS WITH YOUR VOW

**To make your vow call [214] 620-6200
or write:
Robert Tilton Ministries
P.O. Box 819000 • Dallas, TX 75381**

Name _____

Address _____

City _____ State _____

Zip _____ Phone (_____) _____

All funds are used for designated projects and for the worldwide ministry in accordance with Ezra 7:17-18.

ROBERT TILTON MINISTRIES
Miracle Prayer Requests

☐ Please pray and agree with me about the pressing needs in my life.

☐ I have given unto the work of God. I believe He will open the windows of Heaven unto me, and rebuke the devourer from my life, according to Malachi 3:10-11.

☐ My specific needs are:

_____
_____
_____
_____
_____
_____
_____

RETURN THIS FOR PRAYER

Name _____

Address _____

City _____ State _____

Zip _____ Phone (____) _____

Robert Tilton Ministries • P.O. Box 819000 • Dallas, TX 75381 • (214) 620-6200

If you have a testimony of how our monthly books and tapes have changed your life, please write and tell me about it. Send a snapshot of yourself, too.

_____
_____
_____
_____
_____
_____
_____
_____
_____
_____
_____
_____
_____
_____
_____

Name _____

Address _____

City _____ State _____ Zip _____

Phone _____

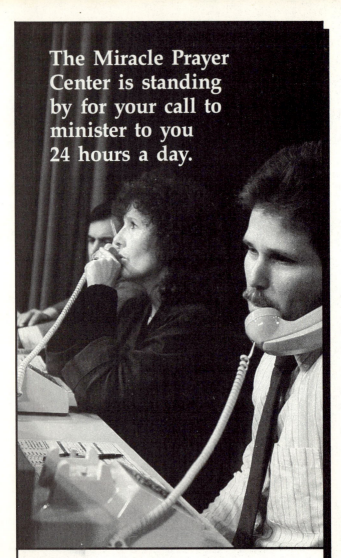